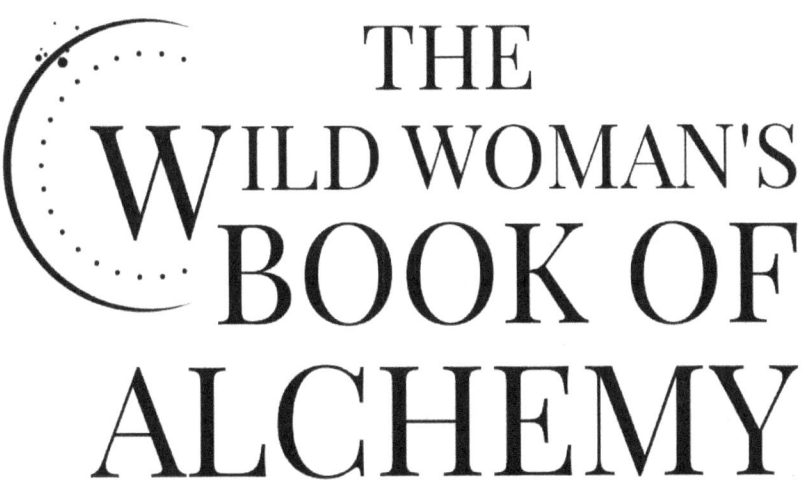

THE WILD WOMAN'S BOOK OF ALCHEMY

A Magical Guide of Rituals + Practices
for Living an Empowered Life

MELISSA KIM CORTER

AND WILD WOMEN FROM ACROSS THE GLOBE

THE WILD WOMAN'S BOOK OF ALCHEMY

A Magical Guide of Rituals + Practices for Living an Empowered Life

Ordering Information: Quantity sales. Special discounts are available on quantity purchases. For details, contact the publisher. Programs, products, or services provided by the authors are found by contacting them directly.

Published by Wild Woman Ink

Book Design by Shanda Trofe | Transcendent Publishing

ISBN: 979-8-218-50635-3

Printed in the United States of America

For the mystical misfits, the ones who refuse to be silenced or compliant. To every woman who is on the path, following the breadcrumbs and collecting the broken pieces, and turning lead into gold. To the wild, unruly, and feral ones sharing formidable magic.

☾

CONTENTS

Introduction

MELISSA KIM CORTER

We can never predict what a project will look like until it finally comes to life. While reflecting on the intense, wild ride that has become this final book in the *Wild Woman* series, I could hardly recognize the person I was at the beginning. Book One in the series, *The Wild Woman's Book of Shadows*, feels like lifetimes ago, and in a way, it was. Parts of me died, as my consciousness took on new forms. An invisible initiation was underway.

Seeing these chapters come together, it was abundantly clear that the process of alchemy had its way with us … not following a typical structure, not staying true to what had been done before, it commanded its own space. Acknowledging a creative impulse, is like flying blindly, not knowing what is up or down. It's impossible to orient oneself; the territory is new and unfamiliar. This purposeful sense of disorientation is uncomfortable if we're trying to hold a vision and follow through with an idea of what the framework should look like.

This book had a mind and intention of its own. I find this true for most creative endeavors, especially those that tug at the heart and require us to give up comforts. Creativity requires tension and countless obstacles disguised as resistance. These ideas are the foundation of alchemical practices; the experimentation requires we take risks and make a mess in the laboratory. It can be a grueling process, to see all the various parts come to life. This book is a result of the women who had the courage to tell their stories. They share the ugly, painful, and vulnerable parts to completely honor the deeper narrative within the lived experience.

As you read these pages, allow their words, energy, and magic to stir you ...

In the Absence of Light

INDHU ATHREYA

"One does not become enlightened by imagining figures of light, but by making the darkness conscious."

~Carl Jung

I t's an effervescent spring morning. The sun is shining bright, the weather is perfect, birds are chirping, flowers have all bloomed and the morning dew on the petals looks so gorgeous. The day holds promise and brightness around. But for Carla, none of this seems to matter. Her room feels dark, like her soul, a dreary and tenebrous amalgamation of palpable discontent. Her environment reflects her despondency, rendering her unable to continue. Thoughts are racing in her mind, trying desperately to comb through forty years of hard-fought existence for some answer to the one question pervading every facet of her mind:

What went wrong?

Her emotional repression had granted her an impeccable image of prosperity. An image which all too common is a tacit symbol of dysfunction, nonetheless, (the image is so powerful even she is convinced that that's who she really was). But the immense deterioration of soul rendered her mentally catatonic and unable to trudge through the plethora of unchecked trauma. It seemed like the world had come to a standstill. Amidst all the chaos, even the seemingly obvious decisions seemed farfetched. Now faced with uncertainty, she wonders what steps to take next or if she even wants to take any action at all.

Does this scenario sound familiar? Many of us have either experienced this or may one day. After striving for so long to display only the ideal side to the world, the side which society deems acceptable, we begin to believe that is our only side. We relegate our darker aspects to the shadows, pretending they do not exist, until everything falls apart. So why does this happen? Is it wrong to be well-behaved and strive to be good? Do repressing impulses and maintaining composure threaten our lives? What exactly are we implying here?

We are here to discuss shadows and the consequences of ignoring them. The wounds, impulses, and triggers that lead us to act in unacceptable ways are often pushed into the abyss within us until we eventually hit rock bottom. Our goal is to uncover the reasons behind those impulses and learn how to bring forth the goodness they hold so we can integrate and release what no longer serves us. We each possess light and dark sides that make up the whole, and after decades of coaching and mentoring individuals on their transformative journeys, I can attest that confronting your "demons," or those darker aspects is profoundly rewarding.

Before delving into the mechanics of this process, let us first understand the concept of the shadow self. It comprises the parts of ourselves we wish to keep hidden because they do not align with our ideal image. These shadow aspects encompass our deepest desires, as well as hurt, blame, shame, and other "unsightly" traits. Our ego shields us from these truths to maintain a sense of safety. They work to suppress these aspects, deeming them unsafe for expression. When we have felt wronged, violated, hurt, or wounded, we may have refrained from expressing our anger out of fear of causing harm. By keeping these aspects in the darkness of our subconscious, the ego believes it is ensuring our safety. Acknowledging that both light and dark exist within us and bringing these aspects into our conscious awareness enables us to begin the process of integration. This does not entail acting upon our anger, but rather exploring the reasons behind those emotions and understanding the root causes and triggers behind them. Instead of internalizing fear, anxiety, and stress, we can bring these elements into the light to be addressed effectively and thoughtfully.

As we all know, shadows exist only where there is a source of light. Hence, shadow does not equate to absolute darkness. Shadows consist of three parts: Umbra, the darkest segment where minimal light penetrates; Penumbra, the transitional shadow with some light; and Antumbra, the outermost shadow boundary. Recognizing these distinctions reveals that the varying degrees of shadow align with the amount of light cast upon an object. When there is sufficient light, no shadow is cast. Similarly, we harbor varying depths of conflicting aspects within ourselves, striving to conceal them. For instance, we may feel self-conscious about voicing certain thoughts or feelings.

The level of discomfort might resemble the outermost region of the shadow, making it easier to address than deeper-seated issues.

Engaging in shadow work is essential because it allows us to unearth hidden gifts that contribute to our growth and authenticity. For instance, if witnessing an injustice triggers anger within you, but due to past painful experiences with such confrontations, you may have suppressed that anger and buried the associated wounds and emotions. Despite believing you have hidden these aspects effectively, even minor conflicts may trigger you. By bringing these suppressed feelings to light, examining the underlying causes, and resolving the internal conflict, you can heal those wounds and embody the assertive, courageous, and confident individual capable of addressing conflicts maturely. Without this introspective journey, you may feel confined in your self-made prison, attempting to numb your emotions and resorting to ineffective coping mechanisms that fail to address the root issue. From personal experience, I can attest that the rewards of delving into these shadows far outweigh the challenges. Even if immediate benefits are not evident, you gain clarity regarding your core values and release that which no longer serves you. This process nurtures both mental and physical well-being, fostering a sense of wholeness and acceptance. Embracing your imperfections as integral parts of yourself allows you to feel complete and whole. Depending on the depth of the shadows within you, the journey toward transcendence may require more effort and illumination.

Each step of this transformative journey proves invaluable, echoing Carl Jung's belief that confronting our darker side is essential for completeness. One cannot achieve enlightenment by simply imagining figures of light, but rather by confronting and embracing the darkness within. Now equipped with an understanding of the shadow and the advantages of this inner work, let us explore how to effectively engage in this transformative process.

Various modalities like Hypnotherapy, Integral Breathwork, NLP, EMDR, EFT, psychotherapy, or energy work can aid in the healing and reprogramming process. Below, I have outlined a few key steps to remember when embarking on this journey:

Awareness: Acknowledging your desires, anger triggers, and other uncomfortable emotions is the initial step in this journey. Shedding light on behaviors or traits that trouble you is crucial for illuminating the aspects within yourself.

Being Truthful: Once aware of what troubles you, it is crucial to be honest about these feelings. The first person we deceive is ourselves. So being honest and genuine about your feelings and emotions may be challenging at the beginning, but gradually becomes a new norm.

Acceptance: The next step involves embracing acceptance. First comes awareness and honesty with yourself. The next step is to acknowledge that there is a conflict within us that we are not happy about and have been avoiding. Acceptance is key in resolving half of the conflict because understanding must precede acceptance. Frequently, we find ourselves trying to make sense of things before we can truly accept them. As a result, by the time we reach acceptance, we typically have gained some level of understanding of the problem.

Resolving Inner Conflict: Recognizing the conflict between our ego mind and our hidden self is the subsequent step, in this journey. As we strive to comprehend both sides, we are also working on reprogramming our ego to establish new standards and perspectives. It entails thinking and letting go of outdated patterns that no longer serve us well. Approaching the situation objectively and viewing it from a new context can aid in resolving conflicts effectively.

Compassion: Showing compassion, care, kindness, and love toward the neglected parts of ourselves is vital. This aspect of your being requires attention, love, and tenderness. Be gentle with yourself. Avoid engaging in self-deprecating dialogues and self-criticisms. The words we speak to ourselves hold significance. It takes effort to heal wounds and transform challenges into opportunities. Remember to be patient and adopt a compassionate attitude toward yourself.

Curiosity: Maintaining a sense of curiosity throughout the journey helps you remain focused and on track toward your goals. By staying inquisitive as you delve deeper it's like solving a puzzle. Approaching the journey with curiosity allows for objective exploration and appreciation of the transformative process.

Forgiveness: Practicing self-forgiveness is crucial in this journey. Understanding that we make our decisions based on the knowledge and resources available at the time enables us to forgive ourselves. Forgiving yourself enables growth and prevents getting trapped in old narratives. Letting go of past burdens becomes easier when we forgive ourselves. Self-forgiveness paves the way for healing and release. As we extend forgiveness to ourselves, we also become more forgiving toward others.

Gratitude: It is crucial to express gratitude for the opportunities that come from exploring our shadows. Understanding that facing challenging moments is just part of the journey, and not unfair, can lead to personal growth. Even though delving into the shadow can be difficult, each challenge we encounter is a pathway to personal growth and evolution. Showing gratitude for the experiences we've had and recognizing our resilience in overcoming obstacles to achieve success is vital.

Celebrate: Celebrating your progress, no matter how small, serves as motivation and reinforcement. Acknowledging every step taken toward growth and self-improvement fosters a sense of accomplishment and encouragement. It's not about boasting. Taking a moment to appreciate and feel good about your progress is essential. Choosing this path wasn't easy. Here you are still pushing forward. Remember, it's not only the milestones that matter; every little positive change along the way also deserves acknowledgment and a moment of celebration. Embrace whom you are becoming.

In addition to the aforementioned steps there are a few more points to consider.

Time: Be patient with yourself. Allow yourself the necessary time to undergo this process. Healing and growth are gradual, requiring patience and persistence. Stick with the process all the way through until you reach your desired goal.

Dissonance: It's normal to feel out of sync when making changes. Acknowledge the discomfort that may arise during the process of change. Adjusting to new patterns and perspectives takes time. Remember the benefits awaiting you at the end of this transformative journey and stay committed. No matter how small or insignificant it may seem stick with the process until you feel comfortable and fulfilled.

Tracking: Journaling or documenting your progress aids in recognizing how far you have come and the accomplishments you have achieved.

Support: Even though your journey is yours alone to travel, the help and encouragement from outside sources such as friends, coaches, and groups play a crucial role in your achievements. Understanding that you have a network of support and love surrounding you not only speeds up the healing process, but also aids in the overall integration of your experiences.

Repeat: Engaging in this process multiple times reveals new insights and opportunities for growth. Each iteration offers a fresh perspective and starting point for further growth.

First and foremost, I want to express my heartfelt gratitude to each of you for your presence and your dedication to embarking on this transformative journey. Whether you're already immersed in this work or just starting out, I extend my thanks and admiration to all of you because this journey is no feat. It takes courage and love to be where you are now. Individuals like Carla, who have persevered through life's challenges and remained steadfast in their pursuit of growth, inspire those around them. Your efforts have a ripple effect, influencing not only yourself but also those in your sphere of influence. Thank you for being the beacon of light amidst the darkness.

Amidst the profound darkness, the faint glow of a firefly can illuminate the path, guiding you to shine brighter than the stars. Embrace the shadows, heal the wounds, and unleash the hidden treasures within you. The world awaits your brilliance. Your journey toward authenticity and wholeness is a testament to your inner strength and resilience. Thank you for being a beacon of light in a world that needs your vibrant presence.

☾

Indhu Athreya holds an MBA graduate and an integrative healing arts practitioner certificate from Southwest Institute of Healing Arts (SWIHA). She is an IT professional, entrepreneur, transformational coach, certified hypnotherapist, NLP practitioner, mentor, and teacher. Indhu has over two decades of experience in self-healing and has practiced and mastered over twenty alternate healing modalities. She feels very passionate about transformational coaching as a way of empowering others and facilitating conscious creation. Her motto is, "Your inner wealth creates external affluence." Indhu takes a logical approach to coaching and mentoring, combining analytical knowledge and spiritual wisdom to help clients create impactful changes and transcended creations. She currently lives in Arizona with her two children. Her hobbies include reading, painting, cooking, singing, and dancing. She enjoys puzzles and mysteries. To learn more about her coaching or to schedule your initial assessment call, please email her at:

team@sukhamindbodywellness.com

Wail Mother

SELEKA BEHRS

She's perfect; her innocence remains an impeccable white light. Her name is Zolstice Mira. She was born of pure love, sixteen years in the making. There was always an "if" – one that grew louder as we approached ten years of harmonious union and I approached my thirty-fifth birthday. Chances of a healthy full-term pregnancy were slimmer than I had realized. All I knew was that for years my body wasn't behaving normally.

In spring of 2019, I received a craniosacral session with the intention of releasing trauma from my first child's passing. I was twenty-one when Zaque was birthed in a hospital in Texas, May of 2002. Zaque's father was an abusive man who drank heavily. We lived in Sin City and our relationship was full of dramatic overtures with lusty make-ups. The abuse didn't become physical until I was pregnant. He cheated on us on Valentine's Day. We had one more HUGE EXPLOSION, resulting in the authorities taking him to jail and a restraining order. Everything about the situation felt gross. I was sick to my stomach all day, every day. It wasn't just the pregnancy. I was detoxing from this tumultuous relationship. As a pregnant mama, I was not going to raise a child with this type of father figure. I knew I had to leave town or I'd step right back in the thick of it.

After fleeing to Texas, I had an appointment with a new doctor lined up and I was slowly finding my way forward. I was planning for a family friend to adopt the child. Before I could formalize the open-adoption contract with her and her husband, I was in labor. It was too late to stop what was now an active trauma to my body, emotions, and psyche.

Zaque was right on cosmic time and too Earth early. The professionals exclaimed he wasn't "viable" and there was nothing they could do. I was distraught. My mother was on her way to hold my hand through it all, but Zaque came and went so fast. He breathed a mere half hour. I didn't realize he was alive until reading the records of his birth and death time. I ached when I saw how long he was there, unheld and unattended. I was phoned a week later by the hospital staff. They told me I had a very curable sexually transmitted disease. They said it was the reason my pregnancy terminated: infected placenta. Twenty weeks exactly. Zaque was buried on the day we were supposed to see the new doctor. For years, I wondered if we made it to that appointment, could we have saved his life?

That spring day in 2019, I lay on the massage table in the office of the craniosacral therapist. I told her everything. I felt all of those feelings move through me – out of me. There was a clear shift into a deeper level of acceptance and gratitude. Zaque chose to save my life. That was his mission and he completed it. He didn't need to go through the arduous life on Earth. He was already perfected. By receiving The Breath of Life, he was ready for the next level of spiritual ascension. This little perfect being came through my physical body and it was an honor. I feel proud to know him.

His personality has always been clear to me. I can see him and feel into who he is and what might have been his future. Zaque has golden blonde hair and deep blue-green eyes, like the sea on a sunny day. He is valiant and persistent. He is witty and wise. He is steady and courageous and ready to war for the disenfranchised. He is a saintly being. What a magnificent angel! Zaque stayed with me energetically as a personal guardian angel – an angel I know by name. He's someone I can connect with because I know his energetic signature.

I wonder what Zaque would be like at this stage of development. I imagine what life might have been like for me as his "auntie." I think he loves music and probably plays percussion or guitar, or both. He is athletic and soccer is his favorite game. He finds solace in nature and he loves being educated in wilderness survival. He becomes a licensed wildlife caretaker and he buys a small plot in the forest to raise his family, eventually. Knowing him like I do created an energetic tether that kept him tightly close to Earth, ready to be with me and assist along the journey. The number 2 repeating is a signal to me that he is with me. I see 22, 222, and 2222 with great frequency.

The grief changed shape each year. I often blocked off the whole week to wallow in grief's waves – to really feel them wash over me. I wore this surfing as a badge of courage. I could do it. I could face those multifaceted waves of emotion. I could make it through the dark storm. My boat was steady on course. The weather was predictable and I was prepared. And every year, grief surprised me.

I sensed he wasn't alone "up there" in the spirit world. I felt another child often dancing around him. Her sweet energy so playful, loving, and bright. All I knew of her so far was that she would be called Baby Zee. I rested prone on the massage table, my eyes gently closed. I could sense how obstinate she is and how much she didn't want to be tethered to Earth like Zaque – as Guardian. I find her energy to be similar to the vibration of Muse. She wanted him to come out further in the galaxy to play bigger energy games. She would circle back to send us beams of love. It would be a big decision for her to come through my channel of birth and live a full life on Earth. It was not a choice that was taken lightly. I realized that I didn't want to do any infertility procedures or have any medical intervention regarding becoming pregnant. It felt like letting Zaque go was the first step in showing Baby Zee, and all of us, that I was ready to move forward with the grief differently.

I brought a playlist of Nordic music that gave our session a feel of a Norse funeral. I watched that unfold in the ethers like an epic movie. The big ship was engulfed by gaseous blooms of yellow, orange, red, and blue. I said farewell to my son and the weight of that grief has been forever changed. It is lighter now. I offered forgiveness to myself, to my ex, to the hospital staff, and to my Higher Power. I found forgiveness by accepting the concept that my son chose this path and this act of love helped me avoid a lot of suffering – misery for years. I forgave the version of myself that kept going back to that relationship. I accepted the hospital staff did the best they could with the knowledge, expertise, and emotional intelligence they held at the time. I thanked Spirit for the blessing of creating life and the lessons that came through the grief process. I held this ceremony with the support of my ancestors and my descendants. And so it was, real and true.

I decided 2019 would be the year I invited Baby Zee to come home. I knew that all I could control was me – my habits – my willingness to create a healthy womb space – my participation in the act of making love; a baby invitation. I scheduled my travel around my cycle. I ate good foods and abstained from known toxins. I welcomed pregnancy through yoga, breathwork, nutrition, exercise, and hormonal support. I was all in – whole ass – big intentional energy.

After the year of effort, I relaxed. In April of 2020, my husband and I went on a secluded vacation to a cabin in the woods and we conceived our daughter, Baby Zee. Two months later, I had an early-term delivery at home, yes –a miscarriage in the midst of pandemic times. The subsequent Mother's Day carried especially tough storms of gut-wrenching sadness, humble relief, and implosive despair.

I held her in my womb again in spring of 2022, but she left before I even knew for sure I was pregnant. My body told me, though. I honored that with camping under the full moon with some dear friends. We mourned Baby Zee then, too. Later that year, during our anniversary month, we created a baby again! (Third time's a charm, right?) I confirmed this pregnancy with at-home tests, discovering the news on winter solstice, December 21st. Baby Zee was on the way and it felt like this was THE time. Zolstice and I had adequate healthcare. We would treat this pregnancy with the respect and love it deserved. I was doing my very best power moves with all of my motherly might.

With such a high-risk pregnancy, my forty-two-year-old body was going to need all the help it could get. Doctors and I were still deciphering my genetic condition and our daughter's passing validated it – hypermobility Ehlers-Dandlos Syndrome (hEDS). Through this pregnancy, I learned so much and I thank her for being a bringer of important confirmation. The science of 2023 was ready to more fully comprehend this situation than what was known in 2002. Her case study is one that for years will be teaching students about high-risk cervical cerclages. Cervical cerclage, also known as a cervical stitch, is a treatment for cervical weakness, when the cervix starts to shorten and open too early during a pregnancy, causing either a late miscarriage or preterm birth. If we had known for sure that I had hEDS, we would have done that surgery weeks before the day she breathed her only breaths. Now, we know. We also know the first pregnancy – Zaque – was not terminated by a diseased placenta, but the same genetic malfunction that made his passage on Earth happen at twenty weeks.

Zolstice Mira lived for a few short hours, and that was a miracle of strength. She was present with us. She was held by her father, her mother, and her mother's mother. Every moment of her precious life was held in constant love. Her perfect body danced its way out of my womb. She felt no pain. She had only peace in this world. Spiritually, I feel reverence and love for the life she lived and how it affects us and others in the future. Intellectually, I can reason with the good of things by celebrating the tender mercies. She was made only by love and through love she passed time breathing, her life wrapped in the warmth of family. The hospital staff were amazingly adept and kind. They truly supported the wellness of both child and mother. They held a standard of compassion I didn't know existed in the medical field. This is a teaching hospital specializing in pediatrics, so it feels good to know the environment for learning is rooted in goodness. Through this event, there was no doubt a feeling of meant-to-bes, even though it was difficult the whole way through three surgeries and the loss of our baby girl.

It has been over a year, and the grief has changed shape almost every day. There are days I cannot go into public spaces because the sadness gets triggered around children, especially those who would be around her age. How do we calculate such a number? Going from "if she had survived birth" date, then she would be a year and a few weeks old. That's not what was going to happen. If she was to survive, she would have had to make it to a survival stage of development – twenty-four weeks being more ideal. That would sum her date a month later. What about her due date, could that be a marker of "she would be this old"? With my son, I was convinced he could have been saved since they did nothing to try. I used his birth-death date – his Date – as the marker. I suppose logic leads me to calculate hers the same, but it feels off. I cannot attach a certain day, though her Date is the start-point of default. My brain brackets it [she would be around a year old now]. We planted lilacs and forget-me-nots in her honor and I hold gratitude for their growth.

Toddlers and tiny humans in public definitely can be overwhelming for me. While I cannot hermit forever, I acknowledge my ability to leave a space or change my interaction with it to accommodate my presently dynamic needs. Their gregarious sounds can be especially grievous. I carry earplugs everywhere, and noise-canceling earbuds. I give grace to my sadness and hold it with care. I know I will have to navigate random waves of grief, so I prepare like I'm going to the ocean.

☾

Seleka Behrs is a Holistic Mental Health Specialist and Grief Support Sound Healer. Seleka is the poetic author of *Wail Words*, published in 2024. Her sound healing operatic musical project, Wail Channels, is a prayerformance art available for bookings. Seleka answers a spiritual call to courageously share her heart's songs. She surfs emotions; swims in them. These waters are where she plays freely as a whale; a wailer. She is not afraid of sadness, anger, melancholy, fear, or confusion. The deep flow's currents can carry us into darkness, and it's helpful to have guidance on the journey back to the shores of contentment, joy, and love. She is a natural guide, following the surges, searching for sunlight at the surface, catching her breath again and again. Seleka's voice wails to other whales, letting them know they are not alone in the vastness of the void. Her work is dedicated to every childless mother and motherless child, and to those who have lost themselves in grief, in love, or in unrequited yearning for a different timeline.

Freedom Through Accountability

ANYA FLETCHER BOWMAN

As you'll see in this chapter, life can be much easier, more fulfilling, and less painful when we take full ownership of it and do the work to heal our current and childhood wounds. In 2010, I chose to end a thirteen-year relationship. We had been married for most of that time, and we were a good team, had several children, and shared a deep love for one another. However, there were things I considered intolerable – things I had spoken on too many times for far too many years – and I was no longer willing to deal with them.

I told my husband that I wanted a divorce; however, there was a separation period when we thought we could make it work by having a "nest home" and continuing to live together as a family (albeit not as a couple). Unfortunately, this did not work and I remained in the home while he moved back home with his mom. That's when I decided to finalize the divorce, which resulted in chaos, thankfully for a relatively short time. When things settled, it was obvious that there was so much heartache, not only for our children and my ex-husband but for myself. We split custody and did our best with divided time to move forward painlessly. Thankfully, he always was — and still is — a pretty great father and did everything in his power to have a (mostly) positive relationship with me for the sake of our children.

For about a year, we continued to spend time together as a family to make this transition as easy as possible for everyone. The following year, however, I spent most of my time with my best friend and sowing my wild oats, so to speak. In many ways this newfound freedom felt so good, yet I realized that I missed my family deeply.

I visited my dad, hoping to find some answers on how to move forward in a healthy way. Specifically, I wanted to know what he did to kill the pain of leaving his children when he and my mom divorced. His response: he filled all his time with work by living in the woods and bringing down trees as a lumberjack. I knew this wasn't the answer I was looking for and left shortly after, driving to California to find solace in the ocean. My relief was short-lived and I quickly returned home, only to throw myself into work, just as my father had suggested, in an attempt to numb out. During this time, I could usually be found doing one of three things: being with my kids, hanging out with my best friend, or working seventeen-hour days. This worked for a time, but ultimately, it didn't lift the guilt and shame I felt about destroying our family.

These feelings were so overwhelming that I chose to leave a loving and supportive relationship for a toxic one. I know this sounds crazy, but the pain was so intense I hoped the punishment would fit the crime and I could let myself off the hook for the devastation that I believed I alone had caused. I also had high hopes that because I had known and loved this person, they would eventually realize I was worth loving, and the punishments would stop. I also hoped we could grow beyond that as a couple and things would improve. Unfortunately, that was not the case, for he thrived on the torture – stonewalling, gaslighting, and playing psychological games, all while playing the victim and convincing the whole community that he was a saint. I was portrayed as the devil incarnate, which he thoroughly enjoyed. Near the end, he finally admitted that he had been happy the whole time, knowing I was miserable, and he took joy in that.

Thankfully, throughout this marriage I had a strong support system in the form of my best friend, who never turned their back on me (though they had every right to), and my doctor, who became more like family than a medical professional. My kids, ex-husband, and clients helped keep me grounded and as semi-sane as I could be, given the situation I alone chose to remain in. The support my doctor gave in the form of energy work, based loosely on the Body Talk, Emotion Code, and Body Code, is what I've found to be the most powerful and life-changing treatment. This work helped me focus on addressing the many instances of childhood trauma.

While healing this trauma, something happened that I did not expect: I started to realize this relationship wasn't what I wanted, needed, or deserved. By 2019, I was no longer willing to accept this reality and decided to end the relationship. I had yet to tell him, though, as I was in school and wanted to complete that before shifting our whole lives again. However, with the Universe as it is, he somehow got the message and came to me unprompted, seeming to take ownership of his behavior, making noise about how "he knows he can be hard to love" and promising to change. And he did change his behaviors, becoming involved in daily tasks as a partner would and being more kind. This lasted six weeks, after which he slowly returned to his usual routines. Just as I was gearing up to let him know I was done, the Universe threw yet another curve ball into the mix: COVID-19. In this space of fear and uncertainty that came for many of us during that time, I chose to stay in the relationship, hoping to at least get through this world-changing event as unscathed as possible while continuing to provide for and protect my children.

During this time, I chose to uproot our lives completely, leaving most of my mostly adult children, my business, and my support system to move fifteen hundred miles away with this husband and our young son. There, I pursued the job I had finished schooling for, throwing myself into the deep end of the Covid pandemic as a first responder. I had never known anything about this world, and the added stress coupled with the impact of the relationship dynamics was overwhelming. My nervous system took a huge hit, becoming completely dysregulated, and I developed PTSD. Living this way wasn't an option long-term, and we moved back home to our families with no jobs other than the dormant businesses we each had. He could jump right back in, but mine was a little more complicated and I struggled.

After a very short time back home, I chose to end yet another family structure. Luckily, after only ten years in this relationship, the feelings of failure and shame weren't present; however, there was a deep sense of betrayal from and for myself and those impacted by my choices. I tried to project those outward but couldn't outrun them or lay blame where it didn't belong. My self-hatred grew, and the grief was once again made so deeply apparent. Internally, I ached for relief, yet a part of me felt I deserved punishment... again. I began to realize that I had been forcing myself to stay in incredibly painful situations in the hope that I could somehow heal them by changing my mindset/beliefs/outcomes with these people and situations. What I didn't know was that all I was doing was furthering my sense of powerlessness, vulnerability, and victimization. When I finally took full ownership of my life and the situations I had created or allowed, I slowly regained my sense of power.

Through this journey, I attempted to be healed through others. I utilized talk therapy, acupuncture, herbs, medicines, and grounding. All showed me some improvement, but none were the catalyst I needed to reclaim myself, my life, and my sense of purpose. The grief and sense of overwhelm had a stranglehold on my heart, and all I could experience was pain and anguish. This was only made worse by the awareness that I had so much I could be grateful for, but instead, these blessings felt like burdens and more pain. My father's death threw me deeper into this vortex of pain I'd been living in.

One day, while surfing Facebook, of all places, I came across a recommendation for the Belief Code, a new modality related to the Emotion and Body Code protocols. Having experienced great healing and growth with those modalities, I was hopeful that the Belief Code would be my guiding light out of this pain and suffering. I did notice a difference, but nothing as life-changing as the other two had been. I realized later that maybe the added grief of my dad's death was just too fresh and new that I wasn't quite ready to return to a place of peace and joy. Maybe this deep, overwhelming grief was truly an honor of the unrealized love and relationship I so desperately wanted but neither of us made happen while he was on this earth. As I continued to struggle with these emotions, some days barely able to get out of bed after an anxiety-ridden, sleepless night, I sought relief in the form of pharmaceutical sleep aids. These left me groggy and exhausted the next day, but the added sleep helped me get through my days. I knew that these, too, weren't a long-term treatment, and I still sought true healing.

I came across a gentleman from the UK who offers T3, another type of energetic childhood trauma healing that I have found profound. This therapy addresses the events and beliefs that have continued to influence and directly shape my decisions, actions, outcomes, and life. It clears the negative aspects of those times and replaces them with a truer and aligned perspective of the truth of who I am and always have been. This has been profound, not only in returning me to how I knew myself before the chaos all those years ago, but in introducing me to a strong, calm, and centered version of myself that I've never known. This allowed me to finally speak, act, and live from a space of authenticity grounded in my truth. It opened my heart to those who mean the most to me and those I chose to shut out to keep myself safe and protected. It allowed me to feel peace and joy in ways I hadn't in years and fully embrace the love. For this, I had to give the love I was blocking in an attempt to keep a distance for safety.

Today, I am incredibly blessed and grateful to be healing and mending the relationships I challenged and almost broken because of my pain, dysregulation, and grief. Thankfully, many of the PTSD symptoms have all but disappeared, and I finally have the energy and drive to have not only a positive outlook on life and my hopeful future, but I am once again allowed to create a life that I love and cherish.

C

Anya Fletcher Bowman is a sensitive and observant individual who attuned to others at a very young age in an attempt to survive. This allowed her to not only develop empathy and compassion but grow and expand her intuitive gifts as well. Anya uses these skills and gifts for her own healing as well as supporting others through their own metamorphosis back to the truth of who they are so they can live a more fulfilled and aligned life.

Anya has spent a lifetime expanding her knowledge and experience in many traditional and modern healing techniques, including massage therapy, herbal and nutritional education, shamanic practices, energetic techniques, and paramedicine. Anya loves to teach and her goal is to leave the world a better place both through her own healing, that of her clients, and the resulting ripple effects.

Reiki and the Alchemy of Belief

ERIN CHRISTINE

She stood at the head of the table, a tiny, ethereal woman whose presence reminded me of a breeze whispering through a field of wildflowers. Her hands rested softly on my forehead, her thumbs gently applying pressure to my brows as she slowly rubbed across each to the outer corners. She did this movement several times, and with each stroke of her thumb I noticed an increasing urge to cry. She wasn't hurting me physically, but something was stirring deeply within my emotional body that I couldn't put a name to. My logical mind was fighting back the tears. For goodness' sake, I was just getting a brow wax, something I'd come to her for countless times! I also felt very safe with her, deeply nurtured, and I always left feeling so relaxed and inspired. What could possibly make me feel the need to cry? At this point, she checked in with me, asking how I was doing. She was indeed an intuitive woman and, in my eyes, pure magic! I responded, telling her that I felt like crying, but I didn't understand why. What she said next changed my life forever.

"God knows when we're seeking."

She spoke with a gentle confidence, and though I recognized the powerful truth of her words, I still did not understand how or why. What was clear was that crossing paths with this woman was no coincidence, nor were her words to me. She had come into my world as a vessel of truth and transformation, and I now come to you as the same. Are you ready?

The laying on of hands dates back thousands of years. It is the tender, instinctual, intentional act of bringing healing and relief to our human bodies. According to Christian theology, the laying on of hands is the symbolic and formal act of invoking the Holy Spirit. By the same token, using Reiki is channeling the very life force energy that moves through each of us, including the man we know as Jesus Christ. Reiki is a Japanese healing modality, "Rei" meaning universal, and "ki" meaning life force energy. Now, I don't know if this woman practiced Reiki, or if she even knew what it was, but there was indeed a divine healing energy moving through her that she passed on to me each time she waxed my brows. In this chapter, I invite you to explore your own thoughts, beliefs, and fears attached to knowing Jesus. I also ask you to open your heart to greater perspectives surrounding the mysteries of our humanity.

My spiritual journey began in my conscious awareness in the spring of 2002 when I was pregnant with my daughter. A profound awakening occurred immediately following my first experience with meditation when the veil parted, and suddenly I was seeing into the spirit realms. This was incredibly overwhelming and uncomfortable for me, but it also stirred my deepest curiosities. I wasn't raised in the church, nor were there any religious or spiritual teachings coming from either of my parents. They each boasted, one a proud

Methodist, the other a tentative Episcopalian. We attended church only once per year with my grandparents in the spring for what I jokingly referred to as "The Big Show."

What struck me as strange, though, as I grew up in this environment, was this deeply rooted fear of God that was growing more potent with each passing year. Where was it coming from? I didn't know God and the only thing I was taught about Jesus was that it was bad to say His name in vain. The energy of punishment and "being bad" or "sinning" was very prevalent in our house. Again, this confused me because there were no formal teachings around God, Jesus, or the church. So, when my clairvoyance and clairaudience cracked wide open after the meditation, I was swept away in wonder. I knew something deeply mysterious and beautiful was happening, but it challenged everything I'd known up to this point about God. The God I knew was angry, overbearing, hypercritical, and deeply unforgiving. I always felt as if He was just waiting for me to screw up so He could lay down His wrath. I giggle out loud as I write this because, thankfully, I have since learned and experienced God to be the most profound source of love I've ever encountered. And, of course, it is, for this is God.

This new pathway soon led me to Reiki. It was a time of great expansion in my life. I had more questions than answers, but I was feeling a peace I'd never imagined even existed. Reiki became the anchor to this peace. A healing practice with Eastern origins, Reiki literally puts total human health and well-being into the hands of those called to it. Reiki is non-invasive and creates a deep sense of calm and relaxation. When this happens, the body will automatically drop into its innate healing space, the parasympathetic nervous system, and cause movement of anything that is creating energetic blocks: toxic thought patterns, unhealthy behaviors, or unhealed emotional wounds, most of which are byproducts of early childhood conditioning. Reiki is a direct link to the language of the body, mind, and spirit. As you become more fluent in this language, you will be able to hear your heart clearly and make decisions based on your highest good, rather than something old and toxic that's been keeping you stuck. It is not a religion or belief system. You need only be willing to receive for Reiki to do its magic.

Reiki empowers the self. It brings light to things that cause us pain. To be human is to suffer. No person lives without the burden of suffering, and if anyone knows suffering it is Jesus Christ. But if we take the language of energy and translate it into Christianity, we can change the entire world, bringing us back to a place where the teachings of Jesus liberate us from suffering instead of shackling us to a fear that someone else told us was real. This is where science and spirituality merge, creating the ultimate oneness.

There's an energetic charge around the language of the bible. A single word has the power to immediately anger a person, while at the same time cause another to fall to her knees in worship and praise. Reiki is a disruptor of that charge. It can soften and shift, allowing for the light of forgiveness and compassion to birth a new worldly outlook, one that understands and embraces the totality of All That Is, and sees the world for what it truly is, a grand mystery that cannot be understood in all its complexity in a single word. I dare say Reiki can be likened to the Holy Ghost. It is the unseen forces at play within each of us, giving new life, new meaning, and a deepened sense of purpose in us all.

Jesus too was a disruptor, an alchemist (perhaps the original one), and a radical revolutionary wielding weapons of faith, generosity, forgiveness, and love. He is the embodiment of the Holy Spirit, as are you. We are all made in the image and likeness of Christ; however, we each come to this life with a different blueprint. Our family of origin and the people our souls choose to cross paths with build our personal foundation early on in our lives. We are conditioned through their fears, perceptions, and experiences. As small children, we take on the burdens of their blueprints and make them our own. We then cultivate our lives into adolescence and early adulthood, never truly knowing our own beliefs and perceptions of this world.

Alchemy asks us to surrender what we've been holding onto as truth and allow for it to take shape into something more beautiful and sustainable. In this case, it is asking you to let go of outdated beliefs that are no longer serving the greater good and be willing to look at life through a new lens. This takes immense courage, and it will not happen overnight. I've been fighting my own beliefs for over two decades. The words you are reading now are some of the bravest I've ever put forth. I thank you for your grace in honoring that for me. I also realize in this moment that I'm no longer at war with God and Jesus. And for that I am deeply grateful. But I don't believe I would've come to this place of peace and acceptance had I not followed the path that was laid out for me, even though it was deemed evil or unorthodox by most.

Biblical trauma and religious persecution live inside our bodies. Each cell lives and breathes the woundedness of our lineage and all the ways they chose to embody it. This is a collective wound. We cannot escape it. But we can disrupt it. We can summon our courage and be willing to let go of a truth that no longer serves us, and was never ours to begin with. This surrender brings us back to the fundamental energy that drives the teachings of Christ, that of love. Reiki is love. Reiki is grace. Reiki is compassion. Can you feel it? The essence of the Holy Spirit is Reiki and vice versa. This may be a lot to digest right now if you are struggling with your own definitions of the great I Am. I honor you in this space, as I have spent most of my life here, sitting on the proverbial fence, trying to make sense of things in a way that felt true and good for me. I believe that Jesus reached for me through Reiki. He knew my heart, my story, and how deep my wounds were. He knew Reiki was the only way to guide me home to Him. And it is because of His unwavering faith and unconditional love that I have the courage to challenge the wounds of Christianity to help others find their peace in this world and create a healthy, life- changing relationship with Jesus, if they so choose.

Like Jesus, I choose to walk a path of humility, compassion, forgiveness, and love. My relationship with Him is deeply intimate and fulfilling. It doesn't ask to be screamed from the rooftops nor defended in the totality of my beliefs. The human collective is birthed through this energy, this love. This is true for me. This is true for *we*. There never was, nor will there ever be separation between you and your divinity, regardless of the path you choose. I am confident that more people would embrace a relationship with Jesus if the fear of persecution didn't run so deep. This fear runs through every religion and spiritual practice, not just Christianity. Not to mention, so much of what we run from with the teachings of Jesus is that it feels pushed on us. It's not that we don't want to know

Him and experience the love we've heard about, but we've been force-fed for generations and that strips us of our free will and diminishes our sovereignty. Free will is a divine gift. God would never take away your right to choose how you make your life holy and good. We all need to feel free to come into the understanding of our unique spiritual journey in our own time. And, truly, by our own time, I mean God's time. This is where the beauty lies. Using your own free will to build a relationship with Jesus cultivates a trust and intimacy with Him that can never be taken away from you, no matter who rises up against you.

Hear this, dear heart: you are and have always been a beloved child of God, no matter your beliefs, no matter your labels, no matter your practices, and no matter your choices. You are worthy of all that is good and gracious in this world. That is truth! If Jesus has been calling to you and you find yourself resisting for whatever reason, let this be your permission to get to know Him on your terms. Like Reiki, you need only be willing to receive the gift of His presence to experience the depth of His love for you. But the best part of all this: you can flat-out say no, and you will still be a beloved child of God worthy of all that is good and gracious in this world.

Are you willing to surrender to the alchemy of your own beliefs?

☾

Faerypreneur **Erin Christine** has spent a lifetime trying to make sense of a world she could not fit into. A storyteller, seer, poet, and magician, Erin weaves her own world, breathing in a balance of human suffering and alchemy. She sees beyond the veil and feels the world's pain. This gift has granted her access to the deepest parts of herself and has led her to her sacred work.

Erin Christine is a three-time International Bestselling Author, Certified Transformational Life Coach, Licensed Massage Therapist specializing in Reflexology and Toe reading, and a Reiki Master/Teacher. For over two decades, Erin has traveled within and around the spirit realms navigating life as a clairvoyant, clairaudient, and empath. Her connection to the Divine as well as the natural world allows her to take an integrative, Shamanic approach to her sessions, creating space for her clients to access their own healing potential.

Her other written works include *Born This Fae*, *The Wild Woman's Book of Shadows*, and *The Wild Woman's Book of Prosperity*.

You can find Erin Christine frolicking among the trees in Fort Collins, Colorado, making friends with all the squirrels.

erinchristine.org

Retrieving the Pieces

MELISSA KIM CORTER

I'll never forget the first time I died. Limb by limb… the vultures tore me apart. The dark velvet of their feathers captured the moonlight, shimmering as they danced around the remnants of my body. Once the picking commenced, my remains turned to dust. After a brief but powerful ritual, my body rose from the earth, put back together anew, in an unrecognizable form. My eyes were open, meeting the tenderness of my elder's gaze. Hovering over me, she said, "Well, that was intense." Tears fell as I tried to process this initiation. Something deeply shifted, like furniture rearranged within my psyche, and I intuitively knew whatever came next would take time to integrate. This day signified my death, and the following years became my rebirth.

As macabre as it sounds, this shamanic ritual is an initiation of dismemberment, a shadow work practice that breaks you down and puts you back together again. In depth psychology, we symbolically equate this process to the breaking down of ego, a symbolic gesture of *re-membering* wholeness through dismemberment.

Nearly twenty years later, the memories of my time in the Arizona desert still potently permeate my mind. For two years, my elder was my apprentice, teaching me her medicine ways, one of the many Peruvian lineages of Shamanism. She described me as *one who could see in the dark* and said my gift was to teach the teachers and leaders how to birth light from within the darkest of places. It took decades of study, practice, and countless hours of client sessions to understand and embody her message. This long stretch included discovering the value of turning toward the things, people, experiences, or circumstances that made me uncomfortable – to stop running and numbing. In taking this required pause, I risked encountering everything I'd fought my way out of. It's humbling to realize everything I believed I had escaped was still there, sitting, lurking, and waiting to be acknowledged. It amazes me how long it took for it all to make sense.

Soul retrieval and shadow work are not always completed in a single journey; both involve a cyclical process of gathering and falling apart, a form of modern-day alchemy. As the name suggests, soul retrieval is a process of reclaiming lost soul parts. Soul loss occurs when facets of the inner self are fragmented or splintered; it feels like living as a hollow echo of who you used to be. The disintegrated parts lack cohesion. Integration is a part of mending the fragmented self, retrieving the pieces to move toward wholeness, and channeling the renewed energy into deeper desires, a critical part of shadow work.

Shadow work comes from the term "the shadow self," coined by famed psychiatrist Carl Gustav Jung. The shadow describes the unconscious parts of the personality that the ego doesn't want to identify within itself. In Jungian work, the unconscious is a part of us that is unknown and, beneath awareness, is a psychodynamic part of the psyche. In Greek, psyche means soul. Shadow work helps us tend to all hidden and repressed aspects of our psyche, including deeply held desires, gifts, skills, and talents that are unknown or unexpressed. We will never completely *know* the shadow because, again, it remains beneath conscious awareness; however, we do get glimpses through feeling, sensation, memories, and triggering moments. The shadow shows us where we are leaking energy, giving away power, through our defense mechanisms. Shadow work and soul loss have various points of overlap. Acknowledging triggers invites us to discover where to enforce boundaries.

Shadow work taught me how to "see in the dark" symbolically; it required rituals and a patient, trusting perspective, as this permits the ego to reorient itself from the outer world to the inner, softening resistance and providing small doses of relief while navigating the unknown. Moving through change is an aspect of learning to see in the dark; sometimes we will be required to go back to childhood to reclaim parts of self, to retrieve enchantment. During my process, rituals serve to give the mind a focus as the psyche undergoes a process of transformation. Rituals are bridges between conscious and unconscious, helping to co-create meaning and stay open as the psyche works out the details.

As a child, I had an insatiable curiosity toward the macabre. I was drawn to strange and mysterious books and characters. I made people uneasy with my ghost stories and odd games. The neighborhood kids grew tired of me dragging them into the bathroom to play "Bloody Mary" or incessantly digging in the woods, looking for bodies or wanting to go in their basements, constantly drawn to the underworld and the hidden dimensions of nature and human behavior. I was unaware that this was a powerful gift, a signal from my soul, trying to show me that something valuable was contained in my interests, awaiting rediscovery.

True, these are not the types of experiences that many people find healing or often encounter on the path of personal development... yet my acceptance of my quirky personality unlocked the gifts hidden in hauntingly beautiful things such as basements, cemeteries, and yes, even death. These dark experiences ignited profound empathy and intuitive awareness that allowed me to become a gifted empath. I held other people's darkness by accepting my own.

When I speak of darkness, I refer to various experiences and psychological states, including the unexplored recesses of the mind, repressed emotions held within the body, deeply hidden desires, and the shadow – the aspects of ourselves we deny. Darkness is a realm of potential; it harbors both creative energy and psychological wounds. It serves as a mirror, reflecting latent patterns and processes influencing conscious behaviors. Embracing darkness through self-exploration followed by integration solidifies our growth as we embrace the dynamics of our psyche. It sounds counterintuitive in today's culture of toxic positivity, yet by confronting the layers of the personal and collective shadow, a subterranean path emerges as the ego shifts focus to the deeper self. This activates healing and we then begin to recollect and integrate the fragmented parts throughout the journey of individuation – a return to wholeness.

Individuation is an intrapsychic process involving parts of the psyche. The psyche is self-regulating, instinctively operating to bring us toward a state of wholeness. The psyche works to advance the soul by reorienting the ego toward a deeper self, drawing attention from the outer to the inner world. In the process of individuation, we are guided to integrate aspects of the fragmented self.

When we learn to hold our own darkness, we sometimes unravel the source of unconscious patterns and emotional turmoil. This process enables self-awareness and the potential for transformation. Acknowledging our darkness invokes and awakens our authentic nature. Through this conscious acceptance, we reconcile inner conflicts, cultivate compassion, and begin to mend the intricate layers of our being. This psychological mending instills a deep and trustworthy sense of harmony and interconnectivity. This is one of the many gifts we receive as we consciously learn to stand in stillness, not knowing where we are going, what is to come, or what will arrive next. This disturbs the ego, the part of us that wants to know we are safe and secure. The ego tries to convince us to act, move, and force our way through an experience... yet the soul is asking more of us. Then we enter periods of *liminality* – the threshold between conscious and unconscious realms.

Liminality is a space of transition, the in-between moments where transformation occurs. Oftentimes, this space is marked by disorientation, a difficult internal state that is sometimes necessary as life spins us around, uproots us, and leaves us so dizzy that we release our grip on the familiar or comfortable. It is normal and a sign of awakening potential.

This period may involve a symbolic death and rebirth – a time of deep change, sometimes upheaval. As the ego undergoes its death (a dissolution also called "egocide"), the psyche begins to reorganize itself; this, again, is an aspect of individuation. As deeply held beliefs surface, we move through the mythic cycles of death and resurrection. This describes the psychological process of my dismemberment ritual with my elder. As you move through change, transformation, or egocide, there will be moments of confusion, times when it feels like nothing is happening. Know that they are; it's just not yet discernible to the eye.

Working with shadow and darkness led to one of my greatest gifts: the use of fairytales as psychological and alchemical tools for transformation. In a fairytale, the protagonist often gets lost in the dark wood, a metaphor for the unknown, symbolizing the ambiguous space between consciousness and the unconscious. They are actually in the midst of a transformative journey, while creatures may help or hinder the process. Willingness and uncertainty are the tools upon the path. How we enter the dark wood mirrors our comfort of psychological exploration – how we confront inner turmoil and face our struggle, suppress our feelings, and engage with the unconscious. This liminal realm demands self-confrontation to expand and retrieve the sacred wisdom in a fairytale, revealing the process of individuation. The dark wood shows us the power of thresholds, the complex spaces between getting lost and emerging with new-found wisdom – a symbolic journey through the psyche.

As one integrates the wisdom – or, more accurately, attunes to the recognition that the soul is integrating – reflection creates space to experience the true self. Reflection is the sacred act of observation.

When integration is neglected, the psyche remains fragmented, and soul loss continues to impact the quality of life. Just as a shattered mirror reflects distorted images, the unassimilated aspects of the self form a kaleidoscope of disconnection... and these fragmented pieces dictate our thoughts, feelings, and behaviors. The absence of integration results in a disarray of inner impulses, each vying for our attention. It breeds inner conflict, stagnating our transformative journey. Unattended shadow elements lurk, becoming potent sources of unconscious sabotage. The discarded pieces of lost soul fragments haunt the psyche, leaving a void that hungers for reconciliation.

Integration requires stillness as we follow the pull of the initiation or are thrown into change. Being with stillness, however, can be incredibly difficult, especially as we are constantly inundated with information. *Hermetic intoxication,* a term coined by psychologist James Hillman, reflects the dangers of constantly being engaged, entertained, and distracted by information without time for integration. None of those experiences contain the essence of what the soul is trying to convey; rather, noise gives us a false sense of security, just like food, alcohol, other addictive substances, or default coping mechanisms. Noise protects us from painful feelings and creates psychological distance between us and the guidance we desperately seek when one tries to escape stillness.

I mentioned earlier how ritual helps us move through periods of change, allowing us to feel safe and held in the spaces of liminality, and then here, we may encounter the numinous – or spiritual clarity. We learn to be between, to straddle the chasm between identities – shedding old skin and embracing the transformative power that is taking hold. Rituals guide us through the darkness of change and transition. Just like the dark moon, this is a time when the light is hidden from our awareness; yet, if we keep trusting and moving forward, we will remember that lunar wisdom runs deep, even when we can't see the radiant light the same way we can during a full moon. If you find yourself in a time of uncertainty, darkness, or change, I invite you to craft a ritual.

Seeing in the Dark: A Ritual

Optional supplies: Water or tea (for drinking), a candle, a lighter/match, pen and paper (or journal), a talisman or symbol, and a piece of twine or ribbon.

- Find a quiet space without disruption or distraction.

- Adorn your surface (table, windowsill, small box, or altar) with the symbol that reflects the theme of your current journey (optional).

- Light a candle, let the light serve as a beacon, symbolizing the hidden path you are now walking… through the unknown.

- Gaze into the flame, taking your time, and breathe deeply (five to ten rounds of breath).

- Reflect upon the transitions you are undergoing.

- Write down the aspects you are releasing and the aspirations you are embracing.

- Fold the paper and tie it with a ribbon, signifying the unity of opposites.

- Sit in stillness for a few minutes.

- If you feel guided to, engage in a ritual movement – dance, walk, yoga – connecting your body to the transformative energies.

- Conclude by offering a libation – water or tea – representing the sacred wellspring of the unconscious. As you sip, affirm your willingness to embrace this period of liminality.

With gratitude and intention, extinguish the candle, symbolizing your integration of light and shadow. The ritual weaves a bridge between the worlds, honoring the transformative process and propelling you toward the luminous light of your inner being.

As a highly empathic, intuitive child, **Melissa Kim Corter** was fascinated with other people's basements. Dark, unexplored spaces enthralled her, and her insatiable curiosity toward the hidden dimensions of the mind led to decades of exploring the shadow dynamics within the human psyche.

Melissa is a Depth Psychologist and international bestselling author published in numerous books and articles; her expertise is the shadow side of the personality. Her unique writing style blends psychology with symbolic forms found in film, fairy tales, and forensics. Melissa is trained in traditional Jungian Shadow Work—the root of shadow studies. She served on the board of the International Association for Jungian Studies.

melissacorter.com

To Agatha, With Love

JADE EBY

Earlier this year, I knelt on the floor of my office with tears streaming down my face, an oracle card depicting my writing spirit guide in one hand, and the Three of Swords tarot card in the other. It was time to admit defeat. I was beaten down mentally, emotionally, and creatively. With nowhere else to turn, I began pleading aloud.

"Agatha, please. I need this win so badly. I need to know that this path I'm on is still the one for me. I need to know that I'm not batshit crazy, that I'm not losing my mind, and that everything I've worked for in the last decade is meant for something bigger."

I should've known right then. My writing spirit guide does *not* fuck around.

Later that night, like whispers carried on the wind, I found myself being led to old projects on my hard drive. One in particular, which I'd started in 2017, called to me, and I realized it was the same story calling to me in the present. Oddly prophetic and timely, there were things I predicted in that story I could have never known at the time. I heard Agatha's voice in the back of my head telling me why it was the story I needed to write, *right now.*

As I found myself falling back in love with the story, the characters, the *why*, I also found myself recognizing the magic of trusting my writing spirit guide to give me the answers I need (when I ask for their help.)

When I first heard the concept of a writing spirit guide, I was sure I already knew mine. I had always revered Maya Angelou as a writer and believed that we would be connected in this beautiful, magical way as well.

Fast forward to the visualization to meet my writing spirit guide and the moment I heard, "Ask your writing guide to step forward and reveal themselves." To my surprise, it wasn't Maya Angelou who stepped forward, but Agatha Christie! She wore a grin and I could hear her, plain as day say, to me, "That bitch isn't yours. I am."

We've been talking ever since.

Here's the thing … our *true* writing spirit guides are connected to us because they have the spirit and capacity to give us what we need when we need it.

I've come to realize that while I still revere Maya Angelou and her work, there's a reason she didn't show up for me. She has her own writers to guide and a set of skills that only they can appreciate, just as Agatha has her own way of working with me for what I need.

The day after I discovered Agatha was my spirit guide, I filed my card reading and came across another reading I'd done the previous year around writing and guidance. Guess what?

That reading had Agatha Christie in the role of "guidance giver," and some of the same cards I'd *just* pulled as supporting cards!

Shiver down the spine. Goosebumps over the arms.

She had been telling me who she was all along. I just hadn't been ready to hear it or receive it. But I sure was now!

Her influence over everything became apparent once I started noticing. And let me tell you, it *never* gets old. Every time I make the connection that it's Agatha's doing, it feels magical all over again.

☾

In September of 2022, I was in North Carolina for a business mastermind retreat. Our group was talking about countries and cities we'd visited over the years. I mentioned that my husband and I had been to Japan – Tokyo, to be exact – as that was the number one place my husband wanted to visit. They asked me where my number one place was and I replied, Dublin, Ireland. We hadn't yet made it there for a variety of reasons, the biggest being COVID.

A day after I got home from North Carolina, I was checking my email and saw an invitation to apply to a writing workshop… in Dublin, Ireland… that was taking place ON my birthday…with an author whose books I'd read and devoured. I had no idea he even taught workshops!

I read the submission requirements and the deadline to apply (it was coming up quickly). Then I read the applicant acceptance numbers and saw they were only taking nine people.

My mind went through a series of thoughts:

OMG! This is fate; I should apply!

There's no way I could get in.

OMG, this could be *it,* though!

I don't have anything good enough to get in!

What if I *did* get in, though?

What do you have to lose?

The answer was clear: nothing.

I really had nothing to lose by applying. It was the first time in my adult life that my confidence and trust in something bigger than me trumped my fear. I heard a voice in the back of my mind say, "You *have* to do this."

That voice was Agatha. And she had orchestrated everything perfectly.

On October 27th, nearly a month after I applied, I got my acceptance letter.

But the signs from Agatha aren't always big and life-changing like a Dublin Workshop; it's more often on a much smaller scale.

☽

This past summer, I was stressing out about a decision I had to make regarding a workshop/retreat. The rub was that I'd already signed up, paid for, and said I was going; however, logistics around travel and money were not working out. I spent days literally sick to my stomach about it.

Finally, I just threw up my hands and said to Agatha one night, "Can you please just give me a sign that saying no to this opportunity is the right thing?"

The next day, seemingly out of the blue, an old co-writer of mine reached out wondering if I wanted to write another series together. That same week, I got accepted into a mentorship program.

What is true for me is that every time I take the time to reach out and connect with Agatha, she responds. It's not always what I *want* to hear but it's always what I *need* to hear.

☾

Last year, I ran a workshop for my community members on how to meet and connect with their writing spirit guides. Watching my members go through the process made my heart swell. Some found their guide was an ancestral family member. Some found they too had a famous writing guide (i.e., John Steinbeck!). The process I gave them is incredibly powerful and now I want to share it with you too.

Pre-Work

Open-Mindedness

The number one most important factor in connecting with your guides is your willingness to be open-minded. I can attest to how vitally important this is because I did not truly start speaking with my guides until I fully surrendered to the belief that they could exist.

I *thought* I believed they may exist, but if we're being honest … it wasn't a 100% belief. Know that your communication with your spirit guides will almost always be contingent upon your dedication to remaining open to guidance and allowing whatever happens to happen.

Silence is Golden

Getting quiet and going inward is the next most important factor when it comes to working with your guides.

Prepare Your Space

Preparing your space before meeting your spirit guide is essential for creating the right environment for a meaningful and focused connection. By setting up a quiet and peaceful space, free from distractions, you create an atmosphere conducive to deep introspection and communication. Lighting candles, using sage or palo santo to cleanse the area, and creating an altar help to establish a sacred space where you can feel grounded and connected to the spiritual realm is key.

This intentional preparation signals to your subconscious mind and the Universe that you are ready to embark on a spiritual journey and open yourself to receive guidance and insights from your spirit guide. Additionally, preparing your space helps to create a sense of safety and comfort, allowing you to relax and be fully present during the experience. It sets the stage for a more profound connection with your spirit guide and enhances the quality of communication and guidance you receive.

Call in Your Intentions

Calling in your intention for meeting your writing spirit guide is crucial as it sets the tone and purpose for the connection you seek. By vocalizing your intention, you create a clear and focused energy that aligns your mind, body, and spirit toward this specific goal. It acts as a conscious invitation to your writing spirit guide, signaling your readiness and willingness to receive guidance and inspiration for your writing journey.

This act of calling in your intention also helps you establish a sacred space within yourself, allowing you to enter into a state of receptivity and openness. By stating your intention, you set the stage for a meaningful and purposeful encounter with your writing spirit guide, enhancing the quality and depth of the insights and guidance you receive.

Prepare Your Mind & Body

Preparing your mind and body is all about comfort and relaxation. Whether you choose to meditate or visualize while sitting up or prefer to lie down, the key is to create a physical state that enables you to fully experience the meditation or visualization exercise. By being comfortable, you can let go of any physical distractions and fully immerse yourself in the process of connecting with your writing spirit guide.

You should also prepare a beverage, blanket, or any other item that brings peace and comfort to you while you do this work. Having a sensory item nearby sometimes helps deepen your state of being within this journey.

While this prep work may seem silly, it ultimately sets the stage for a profound and transformative experience and allows you to enter into a state of deep introspection, open communication, and heightened creativity.

Say a Prayer (Optional)

This is by no means mandatory and is a personal decision. After the prayer, I try to release any expectations of what will happen next. Know that if your guide doesn't show up how you think it should, it doesn't mean you didn't make progress. Our guides are trying to find the best way to communicate with us so that we can understand them. Finding a shared language takes time!

Initiating Contact

What I've learned is that the spirit world is much like the living world in that there are many paths to the same destination. That means it's up to you to decide how you want to approach this initial contact. A few different entry points:

- Meditation

- Guided Visualization

- Pathworking

- Automatic Writing

- Oracle and Tarot Decks

Whichever method you prefer should yield similar results – it's all about how you connect with the spirit world in a way that works for you.

Once you have your entry point figured out, it's a very simple and straightforward conversation that begins with:

"I invite my writing spirit guide to step forward."

Don't get discouraged if you don't sense your writing guide – it may take you several attempts to make contact. I've been practicing visualization for three solid years and am just NOW starting to sense my guides. Practice makes progress. And you may need to try a few different things in your mind's eye until one technique sticks.

Explore the Gifts Your Writing Guide Gives You

You might be wondering how you might work with your writing spirit guide, and though the list is ever-expanding here are a few ways you might do so:

- The development and process of fiction or nonfiction writing projects
- Help with whatever writing blocks you might be experiencing
- Writing through or about trauma
- Inspiration for your creativity
- Introspection and exploration of the self
- Help with the process of publication or getting an agent/ book deal

However you decide to work with your guide, remember that they are on your side. They may not always give you what you *want* but they will always give you what you *need.* Connecting with your writing spirit guide can be a profound experience, and my hope for you is that you find support and guidance by working with a guide that has been waiting for you all along.

☾

Jade Eby is an author of over twenty books, a word witch, and a trauma recovery and storytelling coach who specializes in teaching individuals how to harness the power of words for healing and growth. She is the creator of the Writing Fiction to Heal method, as well as the author of *Forged in Fire: Writing Fiction to Heal* and uses the process with her clients, students, and other writers. Jade runs the Rebel MFA Sanctuary, a community for writers and is the host of the Rebel MFA Way Podcast. You can find her and more about her work at:

jadeeby.com

Alchemy and the Earth Elements

LISA ELENI

Alchemy, which has to do with transformation or change, has certain predictable stages. I used to balk at change. I viewed it as cumbersome and reacted to it with reticence and annoyance. I could be enjoying today and yet waiting for the joy to be sucked out of tomorrow by something unforeseen. As I have aged, I find myself more pliable and accepting of the inevitability of change, but I always wondered why I needed to go through it. Since the earth plane is a school of contrasts, I decided that rather than focusing on the why I would focus on the tools I can use to help me stay aligned to my soul's purpose.

A wild woman at heart, I revered the ancient alchemists who explored the nuances of using elementals in their experiments to create change and transformation. As I explored shamanic studies, I decided to combine the stages of change while staying connected to the Earth elements (fire, water, air, and earth) to help make those changes more understandable and easier to navigate.

All change has a pattern that we can see in nature and there are healing benefits to being in nature and utilizing its healing powers.

You only need to call on the four elements and will be able to see who you are beyond ego, toxic patterns, and outdated belief systems to give you clarity, release, and connection.

The utilization of fire, water, air, and earth can help you when you feel stuck, confused, or overwhelmed by extraneous details. Once you are aware of the benefits of calling in these earth elements, you can find solace, clarity, and calm in the midst of shifting. Utilizing the strength and power of the Earth elements can also empower you to view change as a gift from the universal elements. There is a clear cycle in nature that repeats in a very predictable pattern. When you look at change through this lens and utilize the energy of the elements, you will find insights, clarity, and a sense of peace that you can repeat during the seasons of your life. Understanding the power of each element can clarify a pattern in your growth; once you know how they can assist you, call on them. What can be empowering is calling on the elements of nature when you know how they can assist you. You are only limited by your imagination. The following are some basics to get you started and give you some guidance and inspiration for what you can create.

Fire

Fire can represent the transmutation of energy, passion, motivation, and inspiration. The inception of a new direction in your life can be sparked by fire. This is a great element to call on when you want to instigate movement or change. When you are feeling stuck or trapped, fire is a powerful source to ignite movement. Burn out the stagnant energy and bring in motivated action. Listen to the inspiration and put energy behind your intentions to get you moving forward. Fire can also be considered the element of your personal power, the source of your authority and integrity. This can look like creating healthy boundaries, asserting yourself when needed, and using your voice. I have often found that when I want to speak, sometimes I just go with the flow and stuff down what I feel I need or want to say. The fact is, loving friends or family really do want to hear your thoughts and support you. Use your inner fire energy to be brave and contribute to conversation; take up some space in a room.

Fire sparks our vitality in the forms of motivation, passion, and enthusiasm; a zest for life and a sense of adventure nourishes our desire to seek out new experiences and challenge ourselves. I have always loved traveling and have had the good fortune to visit many countries, taking in their culture, food, energy, and customs of the people and environment. Trying new foods, spending time with the locals, and exploring their history and passions connects me to something larger than myself. Travel lights a fire under my feet to get out and explore this world; it challenges me to get out of my comfort zone and explore unfamiliar smells and energies.

Fire can nurture your optimism and happiness. Use it when you need a boost of courage and confidence to make your presentation at work or start a new project. Call in the fire energy to keep you motivated and force you to face your fears and do it anyway.

Call to Action: Sometimes fire is used to clear old debris. In this sense, you can utilize fire to burn your words. Journal to a person, emotion, or situation and then burn with the intention of releasing that fire energy from your body and having it be transmuted for your highest good. You can also utilize the fire element to clear the stagnant energy in your home, office, or personal space. I often do this when I notice that I feel heavy or blah when I get home. Consider burning sage, incense, palo santo, or a scented candle with the intention of clearing the air in your physical spaces.

Earth

The Earth and your body are composed of elementals that connect us. Earth energy represents stability, strength, abundance, and prosperity. It is important to be grounded and/or connected to the life force of Mother Earth. Trees filter our air and herbs; vegetables and plants nourish our bodies, contributing to our strength and well-being. Go out on a hike or bike ride. Walk with your bare feet in the cool grass or plant a garden so you can connect with the nurturing earth energy in your food. Think how much prosperity there is in nature and call in that energy when you need to nourish your new ideas or relationships.

Call to Action: Has anyone ever suggested that you get grounded? I was told that several times and never really understood what it meant. I do know I felt like my head was so filled with noise that I couldn't really focus or recall what I was doing. Call on earth energy when you feel like you are not able to complete thoughts that are errantly running around in your head. We have all seen a bird on an electrical wire – they don't get electrocuted because they are not touching the ground. Of course, I don't want any birds to be electrocuted; I'm just illustrating a truth: if you have nowhere for the inspiration to go, it cannot come to fruition. Calling on earth energy to get you grounded can help the ideas come to you and through you, so you can feel into what you're working toward rather than just letting ideas run around in your head. If you are feeling heavy or depressed in your space, bring in crystals or other earth elements to help you manage your energy.

Water

The element of water connects you to your heart. Water represents feminine energy, emotions, and love energy. It is the fuel of existence; life cannot function without water. I suspect it's my Piscean energy, but I use water when I need to feel calm – whether it's swimming, snorkeling, or even taking a nice shower or salt bath to clear my etheric field or help those sore muscles release tension. You can go to the ocean and feel the rhythmic swell of the ocean waves, watching as they are absorbed in the sand, a beautiful visual of emotions being released back into Mother Earth. Water also instigates purification of your mind, body, and soul. Water allows you to let go, release, and dissolve the elements of self that no longer serve you, as well as toxic emotions created through life experiences. At one time or another, we have all lived through some devastation or spiritual upheaval and know that being swept away or overwhelmed with emotions can be exhausting. Sometimes, just a good cry will make you feel better. This release of tears and pent-up emotions helps us move that frustration, grief, or sadness through the body, clearing the turmoil that can incapacitate us.

The waves of the ocean are always in motion, just as we are. You always get to make a choice; you can let the waves crash into you and throw you off balance, you can learn to swim, or you can learn to surf above the waves. In this metaphor, the ocean represents our daily lives. Dealing with the wave has benefits and downfalls, and you must decide how much water you take on and what you want to release. Let the water element nourish your mind, and let the water wash away those heavy emotions holding you back.

Call to Action: Water can be purified and blessed before you drink it. It can also cleanse and purify the emotional obstacles within your life. Go for a walk by a river, lake, or ocean and feel the water on your feet. Drink herbal tea or fresh water to help hydrate your body and move grief, fear, and sadness through you so new, lighter energy has a place to go. Bringing in shells or a small water fountain and other water elements can help you connect with water in your space.

Air

This is the one element that cannot be seen with the naked eye, yet it is vital to human life and a powerful symbol of intellect, communication, connection to your spiritual gifts, and the Divine. Thoughts and ideas that move through you and are spoken to others incorporate the element of air and help you make unique connections to other people and share information. Everything is created from thought and word: your ideas, love, compassion, and empathy are some of the most powerful emotions that unite us to one another and to the Divine.

Be mindful of your thoughts and words. They have the power to bring joy and peace like a gentle breeze rustling through the trees and the ability to tear down and destroy like a hurricane. I have really had to temper some of my self-talk to be more kind and loving so I can bring in more self-love. Be mindful of how you are tearing yourself apart internally! You are the ultimate connection to Source and you will find that when you are kind to yourself, it is easier to be more kind and loving to others.

Call to Action: Air energy can be accessed in the form of meditation or reading inspiring books that lift up your energy. Study the teachings of ancient mystics to help you connect with higher consciousness. Open the windows to let fresh air into your space or stand outside and let it blow through your hair and feel it on your skin to cleanse your aura. You can also bring in bells or drums and listen to chanting or MHz music that fills the space of your home or office with a higher vibration.

Those are the basics of the earth elements connecting all life forms and the majority of energy on the planet. You can use your knowledge of the elements to guide or support you as you are managing different life events. Several ancient cultures connected to these elements in ceremonies and rituals for healing, mindfulness, and to be in sync with the energy of the world within and around them. This knowledge is still relevant today and can be utilized to help you thrive and find support while you gently move through change in your life.

☾

Lisa Eleni is a spiritual heartist, bestselling author, student of shamanism, and mind-body-spirit practitioner. She is the founder of Heartistry and Herbs, which focuses on empowering women by creating a safe space of love, support, and healing through meditation, art, journaling, herbs, oils and sprays, and several self-awareness and mindset-shifting techniques. Lisa Eleni is also an intuitive tree reader in which you draw a tree! This is a unique way to get insights, messages from guides and loved ones, and generate ideas on how to move stuck energy and harmonize your mind-body and spirit.

To contact Lisa Eleni, visit her website:

lisaeleni.com

Season of the Soul

CYNTHIA EYER

When I was young, I volleyed between the season of my Soul and the season of my childhood. Both are veiled in the innocence of Being one's own truth. Both are filled with wonder and awe, with moments that enchant us and bring us to a state of pure, unadulterated, passionate, unconditional joy. Joy IS the love from Spirit, in Spirit, with Spirit as one. I believe this is our natural, intuitive state. As we get older, we forget that we are from the Light and that the Light, with the Divine Presence, is our eternal home. Because we forget, we spend our human life trying to find a way back home without realizing what we seek. Both seasons are where joy is in the presence of Spirit's love, reminding us to never forget where "home" is – that state of Being from whence we came. Both seasons are the outward landscapes of creation that reveal our internal landscape that has been submerged into darkness. What aids us in giving ourselves – and, thus, Spirit – permission to turn the inner Light back on is our creative spark.

On this earthly plane, social, economic, cultural, political, religious, and institutionalized conditioning demands our adherence to certain requirements. The current Patriarchal Governing Institutions have stripped joy from our hearts, leaving our minds steeped in fear of not being enough because we don't have enough, because we are not worthy of abundance or Divine love. These Patriarchal Institutions have removed Goddess, who is seen as the compassionate, empathetic, caring omnipotence of joy, and replaced Her with a masculine, warring God who offers no quarter, no grace, no worth unless ordained by those He has given complete authority over humankind.

We have been bombarded with propaganda that we are all born in sin and must earn our way back to the presence of Divine Grace. It is taught that one reaches Divine Grace through one's accomplishments and acts of penance. The wealthier the church, the closer it is to The Divine Presence, as are the people who attend, donate to, and abide by the laws of said church. Each is now a slave to the church's belief system and measured only by their accomplishments, as evidenced by one's monetary worth, and that accumulation is left for the children so they too are considered worthy. The gift of being human with a Soul connection to Spirit has been degraded to a mere object of possession, removing one's truth and placing that truth through the lens of the Patriarchal Governing Institutions. Should one fall short by the teachings, they are removed from appreciation and acceptance. Where is the joy in this? Joy has fled and been replaced by fear-based hope. A hope that is steeped in the fear of not rising to the relentless need to measure "up." One becomes at war between their humanity and their Soul. They have forgotten who they are and from whence they came.

Throughout my life, I sought to find my Soul's connection to The Divine through religious teachings. To know my own truth, as a Woman created by The Divine Presence, and receive the unconditional acceptance from Them. As a woman whose career was in the warring, patriarchal culture of the Army, I also sought to BE a difference in contradiction to the Patriarchal conditionings. I not only warred between my fear-based humanity and my Soul, I warred with the philosophies of all six religious theologies. I found that all six religious sects told me to "seek and I shall find," so I sought by immersing myself into each sect and bravely posed this question to priests and priestesses: "If we [humanity] are made in Their likeness, then why must we earn their acceptance, appreciation, notoriety, and love through acts of worth?" I never did find the answers that connect one's Soul back to Spirit from them, or in words at all; rather, I found my Soul's connection, as well as my truth of who I am and whence I came, through expressing that truth in art.

All art forms are expressions that turn on the Light; they give permission to the Soul to reveal the subterfuge of the Patriarchal conditioning that has imprisoned all of humankind in the fear of not being enough to measure up to institutionalized worth. The arts bring the light of reciprocal equality to all of creation, freeing the mind of the systemic intentions of the patriarchal ruling sects to dominate over all who fall prey to those conditionings. The arts are where humanity meets Soul and Soul is reunited with Spirit. The intensity of reuniting one's Soul with Spirit is the pure, blissful, unadulterated, passionate, joy that is the unconditional expression of Divine steeped in love. Joy is where we remember from whence we came.

Sometimes, even when we remember, something alters our perception and plunges our Soul back into the abyss of a darkness so intense that what brought us joy is forgotten. We are lost and wander, both physically and spiritually. Our internal landscapes are barren deserts and frozen, rocky tundra from whence no life emerges. There is no more intense darkness as a Soul who screams its sorrow into the abyss, no hope more lost, no wandering so inescapable than a parent whose child has ascended. I know, because my only child, my son, no longer toiled the Earthly realm.

John had served in the Navy and was in the initial prefatory training phase for Basic Underwater Demolition/SEAL school in Virginia when he was in a fatal motorcycle accident. Upon his ascension back to The Light of The Divine, I was walking the desolate deserts of California, not knowing this landscape to be both tangible and metaphorical. I felt I was no longer in this realm. I had an absolute knowledge of what it feels like to hold no need or desire in oneself as a human being. I felt no thirst, no weariness, no hunger, no need to walk, talk, listen, speak, think, stand, sit, or lie down. All humanity left me, and all that was left was the deepest immersion of weightless peace with Spirit. I know myself to have been in the presence of The Divine in that moment with my son. I was given the gift of experiencing his ascension, placing me in the presence of Divine Joy. In my son's ascension, I was graced the gift of my truth in worth to Our Divine Presence. The grace given without having to earn it.

The joy once found cannot ignite even the smallest flame until one is ready to transition from what I have known as a living-death and emerge, pushing through the weight of desolation so that one may once again remember from whence they came, seeding in one's own truth. I was in the In-Between of the closed passage of a single parent of an only child, a woman in the Army, a mother to a son, a daughter to both an Earthly Mother and a Divine Mother, and all the labels and nomenclatures assigned to me in the human realm and the not yet open passage of my newness in a raw, unadulterated, passionate, unconditional truth. My wandering in the liminal space of the In-Between has taken as long as it has needed for me to emerge into the season of my Soul.

I have since learned to use the Seasons as a physical form of landscape to reveal my own internal landscapes as I traverse the journey I have unwantedly walked. I now yearn to volley between the Season of the Soul and the Season of the Child in the youthfulness of my new path as an honored-life for both me and my son through painting and writing. My son will always be my heart, and what lies in the heart is home, and what is home in the heart is one's joy. The Season of The Soul is found in the season of Spring, giving one permission to turn the Light on through creative expression of what is alive in them in that moment. In one's Season of the Child, found in the season of Summer, one finds their truth within the pure joy of just being, without the burdening conditionings of Patriarchal Governing Institutions. There are no labels or expectations. This joy is found in one's own creativity of planting the seeds that bloom into who one is – in their truth in each moment. Spring is where the Soul sits in the heart with joy, and that joy is one's "home."

In my Season of the Soul, I connect with my son in Spirit, and know once again his laughter of a childhood we shared. In my Season of the Soul, I am free to express all that is alive in me at that moment as it springs forth from seeds of joy as I paint, sing out loud, practice sound meditations with only my voice, dance like nobody's watching, let go of ridicule and expectations in my writings, and return "home," to a place of joy in my heart where my son and I reside with the peace of Spirit, with Spirit. In my Season of the Soul, I remember to volley between the Spirit of Spring and the Child of Summer. In my Season of the Soul I am also the Crone, with the wisdom to no longer believe in what the Patriarchal Institutions tell me I am to BE. For a belief is simply accepting another's interpretation of what is truth and making that interpretation one's own truth. Spirit is found most abundantly in the creative arts, for The Divine Presence IS the essence of creation. I remember from whence I came.

We are all on a journey to remember where "home" is and remember from whence we came. In that journey, if we permit ourselves to turn the Light on, we find a room filled with creative ventures of magical wonder and awe. In the magic of our creativity, we become the difference in not only our own life, but also the difference for others to witness. How one chooses to show up in their form of a magical, creative Being is the true gift of Divine Grace. It is a revelation of immaculate regeneration of one's Soul in harmony with Spirit, in Spirit.

I invite you to escape the patriarchal conditioning and allow yourself to step into whatever form of creativity that brings you joy with absurd abandonment. Be watchful, however, that the form does not cause harm to another, be it human or greater-than-human. Ask yourself if it is kind, for if we seek kindness, we first step out in the Being of kindness. Does the chosen form express what is alive inside without harm to self and others? There is a balance.

In giving The Divine permission to turn a Light on in what is alive in one, one's darkness becomes a shadow of hope. The Light which shines through the darkness is the revelation found through the creative arts in the Season of the Soul. Spring landscapes start out planted in the darkness and emerge, reaching for the Light. I encourage you to mock the greater-than-human world and emerge from the darkness, reaching for the Light as you submerge yourself into the creative arts of choice and watch yourself bloom. As the heart becomes the seat of the Soul, the heart finds joy, and that joy is one's "home."

C

Cynthia Eyer's childhood friends were dragons, warrior Fae, and Jaguars who showed up to teach her and protect her when needed. They are now her comrades, armed with the warrior's mighty double-edged sword of the pen. Cynthia's motto she started while stationed in Germany in the 1980s is "Life is Our Opportunity to BE the Difference." Create a difference. Read more from Cynthia at:

cynthiaeyer.com

Giving Blood:
Learning to Love
the Figures of the Dark

CHRISTINA FORBES-THOMAS

"This is not quite what I planned."

At some point, usually around the seasons when the burden of time intensifies its sting and strain upon our lives, we each utter a version of the opening refrain, our souls deeply attuned to the silent song of despair. We encounter our unimaginable, the bare reality of what is. For as far as memory's lens entrusts, our story seems fated on a slope of melancholy and repetitive gloom. The atmosphere of anticipation is tainted bleak. The same old black clouds hang their heads dismally day after day. No light announces the end of the tunnel, no wine fills our cup, no hope breaks the horizon, no promise is borne upon Spring's winds. To boot, this is not merely our individual human experience, but the story of the world's soul – of its animals, fields, rivers, mountains, and buildings; we are altogether disheartened and grief-stricken. Very present is the deeply felt sense of separation from Source, and we are the reed flute with the crying sound for the longed-for place. These sentiments gush the memory with the alleged events of the 1920s when Hemingway won his ten-dollar bet to compose a complete story in only six words. He penned, "For Sale: baby shoes, never worn."

What mortal magic lace those words together—invoking, at once, an image of presence and abandon, fleeting cheer and dire despair. We each have that account, a haunting story that dwells with us. We are exhausted and bewildered by happenings too hard to bear in the fragile womb of consciousness. We question, not only ourselves, but our place in the world; we make penitential urgings: Perhaps I did something wrong. Perhaps I never did enough. Perhaps I am cursed. Perhaps my soul needs redeeming. Perhaps it is just too late.

For Sale: A Not-Yet-Ness

What is this "selling" Hemingway provoked? What are we giving up? What is the infant emblem we have no room for in our inn? What can we no longer bear that we so badly desire to part with it – and, not only part (because we know it has value), but put it up for sale? We are greeted with an imaginal image of a *not-yet-ness*. We might conceive these baby shoes as aspects of the psyche, including the creative potential, and undeveloped possibilities hidden away in the cellar of the soul. In what ways do we sell these precious aspects of ourselves, our potential? What might become if we give them our attention, if we allow them to be possessed by life – if we give them room for living? A vibrancy will emerge. They will give rise to a new vitality. They can then move, transport, and transform. They can induce motion.

Another, more pressing, force is perceiving these shoes as lying casks of a world we have deprived of life, from which we have taken and withheld breath. It is precisely the resuscitation of this world upon which the coming into being and sustenance of our own creative potential and crafting depends. The shoes are the soleless frames of an imaginative way of seeing; they are the uncultivated sense modalities vital for being and breathing in the world. As we come to learn, the shoes are unused. There is the implication that some time has passed, and even more peculiar in the clarity of this image: the shoes are new, but not entirely new. They have only never been worn.

These shoes, we imagine, have been passively passed (down) for generations, de-soled – layers for life's cushioning and softening disregarded, neglected, made an outcast. We have been cultured to see the world and its vast body as a soulless, literal, uninhabited commodity. And we, in turn, are left the same. We have not grasped how to face or move through this calamity, how to notice, acknowledge, imbue, and recognize life in the world, so we, too, may be imbued and reunited with living potential. We feel the cold numbness because the world suffers, and its suffering is projected onto us. We bear the burden of what is ungrieved within and without. What do we do with the sense and scent of death lying at our doors, with the shadows and haunting experiences we struggle to understand?

Soon enough, we find these figures and feelings are not so easily relinquished. They will no longer be repressed or rid of. They persist in the visions of the night and manically manifest in everyday events;

they array themselves in shapes in rocks and taste in water, in ill-nesses, and pathologies. They are always everywhere, and they call ceaselessly. They need to be visited and grieved. They insist on be-coming. They reassert to be released and *realized*. They demand blood.

An Erotic Rekindling

For all its strangeness, to be able to *see through* this experience, to restore aesthetic sensitivity, to free the soul from the confines of lit-eralism, requires being awakened to and nurturing sensibilities – fac-ulties that were always already present, but untended. It invites a new, sensate learning. It demands the cultivation of the imagina-tion, a calling forth and erotic rekindling of the senses – visioning, *insighting*, listening, scenting, a widening capacity for differentia-tion, distinction, and discernment; the ability to feel, make, occupy, and empathically engage with the *eachness* of the depths of the in-dividual person, moment, memory, or thing.

The peculiar strain of looking compelled by this active imagin-ing investigates the deepest and darkest aspects of nature. It is a re-inspecting and respecting of the neglected and making lovingly of this dense abode, a dwelling place, to inhabit the nothingness whilst making intimacy and knowing with what is, that itself turns into a hermaphroditic act of creation through our penetrating feelings. It is perhaps a poetic gesture as Mary Oliver imagined it, a letting go, a tantric moving in and out of experience

to lose myself

inside this soft world —

to instruct myself

over and over

And is that not just what this journey is – an unhurried, love-making instruction into the Unknowable?

The Pelican and Love's Arrow

There is an old tale that tells of the pelican bird whose young brood incessantly strikes her as they grow. In retaliation, she strikes back and, in so doing, kills the chicks. Thrust into anguish and faithfully filled with sorrow, she sits in grief and weeps over them. By the third day, the stench of loss permeates her soul. Moved by love and compassion, she gathers them together, wounds her own breast, penetrating it with her beak, and from this, an abundance of blood flows that she uses to raise her fledglings to new life and nourish them.

A Beautiful Sacrifice: Love Happening

Tending the tale as an image, we hold in vision everything happening simultaneously. There is an afflicting confusion. There is wild pecking, crying sounds, and a striking back at the infants, these new beginnings, lifeless. We are about to learn a valuable lesson as we now begin to pair and pull the laces together on the baby shoes, the image of our not-yet, or the out-of-life, to see the value of not going in too soon to be rid of whatever phenomena so mordantly disturb us. Instead, we tend to the questions: What does this want from us? What do we need from it?

An aesthetic condition belonging to the image is constellated. We detect and discover a pattern of a peculiar sacrifice that is love-making and life-giving – a beautiful sacrifice: the intuitive display of bending the neck, opening the beak, pressing against the breast, piercing and penetrating, breaking open the vessel of the heart for the sweet eternal sustenance, the revivifying drops, the divine elixir to spill over the still potential. As if an invisible hand writes upon the air and instructs us: slow the eagerness to silence the distressing confusion for it is here, often, from which life grows. Befriend the gore, gall, and grief; pay attention and be devoted to it, be interested in it, become occupied by it, until it is felt, until it intensifies something in you – something that causes you to act, something that makes love happen.

Opening the Beak: *Allowing Things to Manifest*

This observation and instruction endow us with an ability to tell – bringing further recognition to the communal aspect of ourselves in participation with the world. The turning of events requires a heart-felt speaking of, with, and into all things, including our despair. It involves a telling of the materials, raw and raucous: this is how, as a social being, I am affected. It is a bringing of the cups full to the table in communion – this is what I have, the burden I bear, the tribute I bring.

Such an intentional, intuitive recounting of our story holds our experiences in remembrance in a way that is acknowledging, and that energy invests our story – feeds it – with new potential to become transformative and liberating. In our telling, each of us together, our stories gather reviving breath from the boundless corners of the world, and with word after word, we engender new life and bring celebration and recognition to the matters of this life. The re-telling facilitates a re-turning to our hearts, to looking into the vast lake of being, to the already present life-giving faculties, a retrieving of what has been lost to us, a restoring of what we have so taken, and a reunion with our powers and with the body of nature and the world. Here are boots on the ground – we become bodily and *blood-ily* present with what is. Marion Woodman, in her book *Leaving My Father's House*, shares the possibilities and beautiful strength of the mediating and survival-promoting aspect of psychic reality.

> It takes a strong ego to hold the darkness, wait, hold the ten-sion, waiting for we know not what. But if we can hold long enough, a tiny light is conceived in the dark unconscious, and if we can wait and hold, in its own time, it will be born in its full radiance. The ego then has to be loving enough to receive the gift and nourish it with the best food that new life may eventually transform the whole personality (p. 115).

Communal Reflection: A *Being-with-ness*

A dialogical convergence is fostered in this assembly of love as com-munal reflection is held. As the cup is passed, we make room to hear the news the world relates: of its virtues, visions, and dark nights – how it groans under the pressure of our inventions and manic ma-neuvers; of its breakdowns and dis-eases; how it bemoans the loss of its languages and its young; how its intentions have been misunder-stood, its body raided and ravished; how it is stricken by the agonies of injustice and chokes upon the blood of innocents and the composites and waste of the impious. Let it bare how it feels, fears, re-members, dreams, grieves, and longs, and the thousands upon ten thousands of years of rage and silence it still suffers. Through rich exertion, let it divulge how though its sensuous spark is to be found in everything, its numinosity is negated, its multiplicious viewpoints disregarded, and its dynamic elements distorted, disposed of, and de-souled.

And we offer a response to the world and all the figures through an intimate *being-with-ness* – attentive and attuned, validating, empty yet noticing and listening from the fluid-filled chambers of our hearts as the voice of the world summons a vibration, causing movement and momentum within us. We hold gaze upon the band-aged place, the wound, the suffering. We take in the world, and in our breathing in the awe-inspiring images, she impresses upon us as she enters us. Accomplishing this, we can gift the world by returning our affection. We can give back to the despair – love's other face – through our devotion, and we mirror love's light and consciousness with the world. This active imagining, attuning, and dialogic activity constitute the making of the soul.

With these happenings, with the turning of tides and things, we come to be affected – to learn and endure in reverie how something before perceived as dark, huge, horrifying, useless, dreadful, and bitter, can become an image of beauty, worthy of devotion – beauty that stuns, stirs, and redeems the soul. Beauty is beheld through the eyes of love; beauty itself summons love. And through love's lens, we see more clearly. Life is restored to self and world. Body and soul are raised up, exalted. The invisible hand writes us again, in ink fragrant with flowers: "May you be given to such things as loving, living, and revelry, as they are one, tangled in frustration." With wisdom's blessing, we embark upon love's way. As you journey, so may your heart hear and hang to the grace gifted us from Mary Oliver's ritual in "Wild Geese":

> You do not have to be good.
>
> You do not have to walk on your knees
>
> for a hundred miles through the desert repenting.
>
> You only have to let the soft animal of your body
>
> love what it loves.
>
> Tell me about despair, yours, and I will tell you mine.

☾

Christina Forbes-Thomas is the poetic visionary behind *Woman You Are Wine*—a sensuous, spellbinding project, soul-making practice, modern feminine ritual and platform that offers women a dynamic experience for expanding, nurturing, and liberating their imagination and a direct, intimate access to an ecstatic dimension of soul, one that is sacredly attuned to the complexity and fullness of the body, and to the deep instinctual nature. This radical project returns the wild, sequestered soul from the intrapsychic back into the world—orienting the work as a revisioning and novel therapy for the collective.

A mythmaker, scholar-educator, voice and ritual artist, Christina's work and mystical writings bespeak the archetypal imagination. Stirred by the interconnectedness of all things, her background in Depth Psychology and research interests spanning alchemy, ecology, myth, folklore, cognitive science, and the arts propel her to explore their bearings on psychological life, while forging and emboldening women to create and capture imagistic processes, take on and tend forms of expression that facilitate psycho-spiritual development and rich crafting for the restoration of community and culture.

womanyouarewine.com

The Art of Alchemical Change and Transformation: Guided Wisdom to Help You Transform Your Life

KAMAL GILL

Welcome to a journey of self-discovery and personal transformation as we travel together on a quest to unlock your highest potential and unleash the power within you. Drawing upon the ancient wisdom of alchemy, we will explore the principles of alchemical change and guide you on a path of growth, fulfillment, and success. Prepare to venture on a transformative journey that will ignite your spirit, expand your consciousness, and lead you to the realization of your deepest desires.

Throughout my own journey of self-discovery, I have come to know that there is so much more in the hidden realms, and yet simple steps can also unveil the mysteries of alchemical change and transformation, to unravel the Mastery of Creation that lies within us all.

In the depths of existence lies the Art of Alchemy, a journey of transformation where the unreal merges with the real. It beckons us to delve into the essence of our Being, questioning the stories we've been told and embracing the boundless potential within.

Alchemy is not merely the pursuit of transmuting base metals into gold, but a profound metaphor for the inner transformation of the human Soul. As we unravel the enigma of alchemical transmutation, we create practical application in our search for self-realization and success.

I too have journeyed into the realms of beyond and have harnessed a passion for writing and alchemical transference. It is the ability of being able to see beyond the parameters of change and harness the fortitude that lies in waiting. Creativity and Stillness are the anchors I have found that create rapid transformation and I invite you to explore the *Essence of your Being* as we journey together in discovery.

The Process of Alchemical Change and Transformation

Step 1: Know Thyself

At the heart of personal transformation lies the fundamental understanding of who you truly are. In this step, we delve deep into the essence of your Being, peeling away the layers of conditioning and societal constructs to reveal the truth of your authentic Self.

Through self-reflection, introspection, and self-awareness, you gain insight into your strengths, desires, and fears. By embracing your true essence and letting go of self-imposed limitations, you open the door to limitless possibilities and pave the way for pro-found personal growth and transformation.

Intuitive Prompt:

Imagine a journal filled with the stories of your life – the triumphs, the challenges, the moments of joy and sorrow. As you reflect upon these pages, you begin to notice patterns and themes emerging, re-vealing insights into your true essence. You realize that self-aware-ness is the key to personal transformation, empowering you to un-derstand every step that has brought you here. Through this process of self-discovery, you gain appreciation and acceptance, guiding you toward a life of purpose and fulfillment.

Guided Action Step:

- Start a daily journaling practice to explore your thoughts, feelings, and experiences.

- Set aside daily quiet time so you can reflect on your day.

- Create sacred space and set your intentions as you begin.

- Write freely and without limitation or editing.

- Notice any patterns or insights that emerge.

By consistently engaging in this practice, you will deepen your self-awareness and gain empathy for your quintessential self.

Intuitive Insight:

Journaling allows you to connect deeply with your thoughts and emotions, helping you identify patterns and triggers that may be holding you back, or offer insights as to where you are being led. By regularly reflecting on your experiences, you appreciate the paradox of life, empowering you to listen deeply to the voice of your authentic self.

The Transformation:

Your daily journaling practice will help you deepen your self-awareness, opening the pathways to possibility and inspiration, and help you make conscious choices aligned with your authentic Self. Over time, you will develop a greater sense of purpose and fulfillment, leading to a more meaningful and fulfilling life.

Step 2: Embrace Creativity

Transformation requires a willingness to explore new ideas and approaches, to think outside the box, and to embrace the creative impulse that flows through you.

The journey of creative exploration guides you to awaken your innate intuitive abilities, and creativity itself awakens the Still Point of Creation that lies dormant within. It is how you open the neural pathways for more. Whether through artistic expression, creative ideas, or innovative problem-solving, creativity helps you harness the power of your imagination to manifest your dreams into reality and awakens your utmost potential for success.

Intuitive Prompt:

Picture yourself standing before a blank canvas, a palette of vibrant colors at your fingertips. As you dip your brush into the paint, you feel a surge of creative energy coursing through your veins. With each stroke, you infuse the canvas with the essence of your being, expressing yourself in ways you never thought possible. You realize that creativity is not just about making art; it's about tapping into intuitive intelligence that guides you toward new possibilities and opportunities.

Guided Action Step:

- Engage in any creative activity that brings you joy and inspiration.

- Whether it's painting, writing, dancing, or playing music.

- Give yourself permission to try something new.

- Explore your creative side without judgment or inhibition.

Allow the process of creation to be a means of self-expression and self-discovery, tapping into the infinite potential that lies within you.

Intuitive Insight:

Creativity births innovation, intuition, and imagination. By engaging in creative activities, you stimulate your imagination, expand your horizons, and cultivate a sense of curiosity and wonder. Creativity also serves as a powerful outlet for self-expression, allowing you to connect with your emotions and experiences in meaningful ways.

The Transformation:

As you embrace and channel your creative spark, you unlock new potentials and possibilities that stimulate your imagination to seek out new opportunities. Engaging creative expression stimulates the brain and increases neuroplasticity, leading to improved memory and better cognitive function, and also helps you regulate your emotions, which inevitably leads to a happier state of being.

Step 3: Practice Mindfulness

Success is not merely the achievement of external goals but also the realization of inner growth and fulfillment. As we explore the importance of cultivating mindfulness and presence in your daily life, pay attention to your thoughts, emotions, and actions.

By staying grounded in the present moment, you become more attuned to the opportunities and possibilities that surround you, allowing you to make informed decisions and navigate challenges with clarity and confidence. Through mindfulness practices, gratitude exercises, and emotional check-ins, you will deepen your awareness of Self and the world around you, paving the way for profound personal transformation and growth.

Intuitive Prompt:

Imagine sitting in a quiet room, surrounded by the gentle hum of nature and the soft glow of candlelight. As you close your eyes and take a deep breath, you feel a sense of peace and tranquility wash over you. In this moment of stillness, you become aware of your thoughts, emotions, and sensations, observing them without judgment or attachment. You realize that mindfulness is not just about being present; it's about cultivating awareness and acceptance of the present moment, allowing you to navigate life with grace and ease.

Guided Action Step:

- Practice mindfulness through activities such as meditation, yoga, or mindful breathing.

- Set aside time each day to quiet your mind and connect with the present moment.

- Observe your thoughts, emotions, and sensations with love and empathy.

- Create daily moments of gratitude by writing down three things you are grateful for each day, to shift your perspective to abundance and enhance your overall well-being.

By nurturing awareness in this way, you develop a greater sense of peace and understanding, leading to more unity, harmony, and co-creation.

Intuitive Insight:

Mindfulness promotes mental acuity, emotional resilience, and inner balance. By practicing mindfulness, you train your mind to focus on the present moment, reducing stress, anxiety, and negative thinking patterns. Dropping from your head into your heart creates a deeper connection with yourself and others, stimulating empathy, compassion, and emotional intelligence.

The Transformation:

By expanding your awareness through mindfulness practices and tapping into heart coherence, you reduce stress, increase mental agility, and enhance emotional resolve. As you develop a greater sense of peace and balance, you allow grace and ease to be your guiding Light.

Step 4: Finding Stillness

In the constant humdrum of life, it is essential to carve out moments of stillness and quiet reflection. The transformative power of stillness helps you cultivate inner peace, tranquility, and balance.

Through meditation, deep breathing exercises, and spending time in nature, you learn to quiet the mind, soothe the soul, and tap into the wisdom that lies dormant within. By embracing the power of stillness, you unlock the secrets of personal transformation and embark on a journey of profound self-discovery.

Intuitive Prompt:

Close your eyes and imagine you are standing on the shore of a tranquil lake, the water shimmering in the soft light of dawn. As you breathe in the crisp morning air, you feel a sense of calm and serenity wash over you. In this moment of stillness, you become aware of the beauty and wonder of the natural world, allowing yourself to be fully present and at peace. You realize that stillness is not just about being quiet; it's about finding inner peace and tranquility amidst the odyssey of life.

Guided Action Step:

- Create a daily ritual of stillness and quiet reflection to recharge and reconnect with yourself.

- Set aside time each day to unplug from technology and rebalance your internal systems.

- Find a quiet space, and engage in practices such as meditation, deep breathing, or spending time in nature.

- It is in this sacred space of inner quietude that the treasures of Alchemy await, patiently seeking your discovery.

By embracing Stillness in this way, you will create inner peace and the space to self-reflect.

"For what you are seeking, is always seeking you in return."

Intuitive Insight:

Stillness calms the mind, recalls the soul, and restores balance to the body. As you give yourself space to rest, recharge, and replenish your energy, Stillness allows you to tap into your inner wisdom and intuition, guiding you toward greater clarity, purpose, and direction in life.

The Transformation:

By embracing Stillness as a daily practice you experience greater peace, stability, and a deeper connection with your sense of Self. As you learn to quiet the mind and listen to your Soul, you can tap into your inner wisdom, leading to a deeper sense of well-being and fulfillment.

Step 5: Embody Mastery

As we traverse the labyrinthine paths of personal transformation, we emerge as masters of our destiny. As we explore the Essence of Mastery, we offer practical strategies and techniques to help you embody your highest potential and achieve your greatest success.

By creating clear steps, taking embodied action, and embracing the fullness of you, you unlock the keys to personal mastery and unveil the full power of your Being. With each step, you move closer toward the realization of your deepest desires and the fulfillment of your highest potential.

Intuitive Prompt:

Imagine standing at the summit of a majestic mountain, the wind in your hair and the sun on your face. As you gaze out at the breathtaking panorama below, you feel a sense of awe and wonder wash over you. In this moment of imagination and inspiration, you realize that mastery is not just about achieving external success; it's about embodying your highest potential and living your life with purpose and passion, having connected to the Innate Self within.

Guided Action Step:

The Embodiment of Mastery is the connection to Self. By creating moments of pause and ponder and self-reflection, and bringing in the aspects of creative self-expression, you enable heart coherence to be the guiding Light that anchors the Self even deeper, within.

- Review your journey and write out what you want to embody, and what steps you will take to create this version of you.

- Release what no longer serves you, and affirm what you wish to learn, discover, or re-create anew.

- Create clear guidelines and take consistent action toward their achievement.

- Curate the vision and begin taking daily action, and you will empower yourself to create the life of your dreams and activate your highest potentials for success.

Know that the more you are in alignment to what you do want, without attachment, *yet the awareness that all things are done through you,* you will empower the energy vortex to be manifested into form through you.

Intuitive Insight:

You are Creator within your own Creation. You have infinite potential within you and you are here as Leaders and Lightworkers to lead the way. As you create a greater sense of purpose and intention for your life, your journey serves as a touchstone for personal growth and expansion.

As you Embody the Mastery of your own Creation, you tap into the portals of possibility that open the pathway for a more unified world for all. As you channel your energy and resources for the good of The All, you enable even more unity and harmony to be birthed here.

The Transformation:

By consciously creating your life and taking aligned action, you can achieve greater success, fulfillment, and happiness. You develop a sense of purpose and fortitude that empowers you to overcome obstacles and urges you to create the life of your dreams. With each step you take toward Mastery, you unveil your highest potential and you embody the greatness that lies within.

Transformational Takeaway

As you embark on this journey of personal transformation, remember the power to change your life is already within you. You are already *whole perfect and complete,* and by coming to Stillness and creating more moments to pause and ponder, you allow the vibrations of change to filter through you.

With each step you take toward your own transformation, you move closer towards self-realization, and thus, you are more able to co-create the highest possible versions of you. As you embrace change and growth with ease and fortitude, you unleash the potential that lies deep within.

As you learn to embrace all the facets of you, you will see that belief was the thought you kept thinking, and yet your untapped potentiality is what has brought you here. The possibilities are endless, and the only limit is your imagination. So dream your dream and know that you can manifest it all by **who and how you are Being** in each moment of your experience.

- Know Thyself is the first step.

- Embrace your Creativity

- Practice Mindfulness

- Create moments of Stillness

- Embody the Master that you are

- For you are Creator within your own Creation, and the power to transform your life truly does live Within.

Believe in yourself, trust in the process, and let your Light shine brightly for all the world to see.

True Alchemical Transformation is knowing who you are, as you blend all the facets of you, as you mirror your highest potential into form. The Power is Within.

Your purpose is to shine as brightly as you can, and that my dear friend, is how you transform everything around you too. Remember, the power to transform your life truly does lie in your hands, *and it all begins Within.*

Welcome, Dear Alchemist, time to create Magick!

Kamal Gill is well versed in the axioms of life and has the gift of being able to see beyond the parameters of change that affect our everyday beliefs. A former corporate manager turned mentor, author and intuitive channel, Kamal has been supporting human transformation for over thirty years, creating safe containers for people to explore and uncover their hidden potential.

As a transformational coach, akashic records reader, certified mind-body-spirit practitioner, reiki energy intuitive and Master Channel, Kamal offers wisdom teachings and deep insight from the quantum field, and is passionate about supporting people to learn more about who they truly are. She loves helping people to seek this wisdom for themselves and her work serves to raise the vibrational consciousness of our planet.

When she's not writing or channeling new quantum codes, Kamal loves spending time with her family exploring the great outdoors and loves creating delectable dishes that delight the palate and satiate the Soul. She believes *"Spirit is in the details"* and aims to create and inspire wherever she goes.

kamalgill.com

Transformation

SANDY HANSHAW

As a child, I woke almost every night crying or screaming for my brothers or dad to come to my room. I would have horrible nightmares about dead people, hearing things in my head when no one was there, and other unusual things. The most memorable dreams I had were about snakes. A massive white snake was under the blanket, and if I moved, it would squeeze me to death. A dark snake, even bigger than the white one, was under the bed, and I thought if I put my feet on the floor, it would grab me and pull me under there with it. These dreams were so real and vivid, I thought they were actually happening.

These dreams paralyzed me in many ways. Obviously, I was not a fan of snakes and literally thought all snakes wanted to harm me. Even scarier, I began to struggle with what was happening in my dreams versus real life. I often found myself living in an imaginary world or daydreaming, and it was not uncommon for me to hear, "Sandy, come back to Earth," because I was so dazed out. I noticed it happened a lot at mealtimes and around certain people in my life.

Then, when I was twelve or thirteen, my family moved, the vivid dreams stopped ... and everything else ramped up.

My spiritual gifts started coming forward in full force; it was overwhelming, and I did not have anyone to ask or talk to about it. I didn't understand what was happening, and I was scared to tell anyone because I wanted to have friends and feel "normal." My teenage years were trying to a degree, with all of the information rolling around in my head and voices that apparently only I could hear. I was also able to feel other people's emotions. Nothing was worse than feeling like someone didn't like me, even though they didn't know who I was.

After sneaking some beers from the fridge, I soon figured out how to stop it all. Alcohol would numb it all out so I didn't experience the chaos in my mind; I also didn't have the vivid dreams. Later in life, however, I realized that alcohol created a lot of other issues I didn't need to deal with.

It took me years to finally understand that what I was running from could actually be something beneficial – if I took the time to learn and understand my gifts. I started working toward releasing the judgment, expectation, and shame I placed on myself; I made the decision to learn how to heal myself and step into my gifts. I had a new outlook on life and realized just how much of my life I was blindly walking through without any joy or real enthusiasm. There was a distinct shift as I released rules I had placed on myself and allowed others to put on me. I made the conscious choice to live in the present with purpose and to change my imperfect, pain-filled existence into something magical and exquisite. I adopted the mind-set of accepting myself for who I was rather than who I thought everyone wanted me to be.

Of course, this was not without challenges; along the way, I lost most of my friends and family connections and had to grieve them, as well as the person I used to be. On the other hand, seeing people for who and what they were allowed me to choose whether I wanted them in my life or not. Let me tell you, it is not easy placing bound-aries on people who have had unlimited access to your energy or having to release them from your life. It was even harder to release family because they refused to respect those boundaries.

The shift has been literally life-changing. The people in my life are genuinely happy I am in theirs; my dream of opening my own business has come true, and I feel more alive than ever since I started trusting myself and my inner guidance. The first thing I needed to do, however, was forgive myself and stop allowing others to put their "stuff" on me. I want to share some things that have allowed me to level up while finding my authentic self.

The first thing is making yourself a priority in your own life. This can be the hardest step of the process as we have been pro-grammed to put other people's needs in front of our own, especially if you are married and/or a parent. Sometimes we have to de-pro-gram the core beliefs instilled in us as children in order to move forward as adults. My own path was filled with guilt, shame, and feelings of being selfish as I made efforts to heal myself and make myself a priority. What I learned was that if I didn't put myself first, I would continue to feel empty, lost, and resentful of the people I loved the most. It was only when I created the boundaries and honored them that I became a better human to everyone in my life. My relationships deepened, I no longer had the drive to compete with others, and I truly started to feel comfortable in my own skin. Next, I want to share things you can do as you embark on or continue your own spiritual adventure.

Everything within us – heart, mind, body, and soul – is connected, and only we can control ourselves and the level of commitment we have to getting what we want. When we start to trust our soul and our inspirational guidance, we begin the process of spiritual awakening. As we grow spiritually, it is common to outgrow people, places, jobs, and our view of material things. New opportunities, people, and interests that align with our growth naturally come into our lives. I cannot tell you how many amazing friends I have met in social media groups who I've never met in person and yet feel like I've known for years.

Let's go over some of signs of a spiritual awakening. This is not a definitive list but rather common things many people could experience.

- Shift in food preferences; things you used to love are no longer your favorites.

- Sleep patterns shift from maybe being a night owl to getting up early every morning and wanting to be in bed early in the evening (or the other way around).

- Relationships change by either deepening the bond with someone or realizing they are no longer willing to grow in the relationship, and they fade away.

- Intimacy in relationships can change, and likely, they deepen, and there could be a yearning for deeper sexual intimacy as well.

- Inspiration and creativity can surge through you to change things up, declutter your space, and simplify your life.

- Increased awareness of your thoughts, feelings, and actions, as well as even more alertness and awareness of body language and what is *not* being said in situations.

- Intuition, synchronicity, enhanced psychic abilities, and challenges with electronic items

- Depression, migraines, headaches, anxiety, or panic attacks

Navigating a spiritual awakening is unique to each individual; however, I have included some tools to assist you on your learning path. Meditation, energy work, affirmations, and gratitude jars or journals are great starting points.

Meditation is one of the easiest ways to move your spiritual growth forward, yet it is also one of the things people put off the most. We get into our heads thinking about how hard it is to meditate when, in reality, it can be simple. Meditation is about being present in the moment; you do not need to do a big ritual or have any items to meditate. There are multiple ways to meditate; I have found excellent meditations on YouTube, so search and find what works for you. Some ideas that you can learn more about are chanting, shamanic drumming, solfeggio frequencies, and guided meditations. My personal favorite is going for a walk or sitting in nature. Nature provides sounds, sights, smells, and a sense of calmness that is hard to create anywhere else. You are able to focus on what is happening in the moment as all of your senses engage and encourage you to be in the present.

If you struggle with quieting the mind and releasing the day when you meditate, put the thought on a cloud, watch it drift away, and tell it to come back to you after you are done. Consistent meditation allows you to become aware of your feelings and sensitivity to energies while tapping into your intuition. Often people are able to start feeling or sensing energies and how others make them feel so they can be more deliberate about who they surround themselves with. We all have the ability to connect to the Universe; we just need to learn how to listen and recognize the signs.

Reiki and other energy healing modalities is another great way to clear and move energy throughout your body, along with having a daily energy grounding practice. Energy work is a holistic practice where healers channel universal life force into the body to restore the flow, balance, and harmony. Energy work can typically be done in person and/or over distance, based on the practitioner. If you cannot find an energy practitioner in your area, I recommend looking into taking some energy courses to learn how to do it yourself.

Daily affirmations and gratitude journals allow us to stay present while calling in what we want to manifest in our lives. When using affirmations, I like to use the "3x6x9" method. Determine what you want to call into your life. Write it on a piece of paper or put it in the notes section of your phone so you don't forget it. Say the affirmation out loud three times in the morning, six times midday, and nine times at night. If you really want to see some change in your self-acceptance, look yourself in the eyes in a mirror and say,

"I love you" ten times every morning, afternoon, and evening. Another great way to get affirmations is by using an app on your phone; it will deliver them to you based on what you have selected you are working on.

Another of my favorite things to do is write down something awesome about my day on a Post-it note and put it into a jar every night. On New Year's Eve, I open them all, which allows me to move into the new year full of gratitude for everything in my life. I also feel so empowered and appreciative of how great things are in my life while opening each note. This can also be done more regularly, like monthly or quarterly.

Admittedly, I have a bit of a problem collecting journals with smooth, thick paper and quality bold black pens. I use them as gratitude journals, which allows me to justify buying them as I write in them consistently. I write down my thoughts, always starting with the intention of what I am grateful for; however, it is not uncommon for them to become automatic writing sessions too.

The last thing I want to touch on is forgiveness of our own mistakes. This is a big challenge for many people as we replay prior mistakes over and over in our heads with different scenarios and potential outcomes, often making it much worse than what it was. Allow yourself permission to forgive yourself, knowing the best decision was made based on the information available at the time. A lesson I learned in life is that nobody really cares what we are doing as they are worried about themselves.

Everyone's journey is different, and it is meant to be. Life would be so boring if we all did and liked the same things. Lean into the moments of inspiration as your soul is giving you guidance. Do it your way with a personal flare and allow yourself permission to have fun on the adventure of life.

☽

Sandy Hanshaw is the owner of The Sacred Owl and Salt Room in Knoxville, Tennessee. She is also a bestselling author, Intuitive Soul Coach, Reiki Master Teacher, Integrative Healing Arts Practitioner, and Empowerment Retreat Planner. Sandy is passionate about assisting others to find their purpose and truth through education and self-discovery while using her unique combination of humor and intuitive gifts to provide practical guidance. Sandy holds a Bachelor of Metaphysical Science and has more than thirty certifications, including Usui Reiki Master/Teacher, Transpersonal Life Coach, Mindfulness Guided Imagery and Meditation Facilitator, and Certified Belief Clearing Practitioner. She offers her gifts as an intuitive to clear and balance stagnant energy while empowering clients to find the best version of themselves. She is currently pursuing her doctorate in Metaphysical Counseling.

Sandy loves to travel to new places, meet new people, spend time with family and friends, and have a good girl's weekend. She lives in Oak Ridge, Tennessee, with her husband and fur babies.

thesacredowlandsaltroom.com

Soul Retrieval:
Magical Weavings and Gardens

KARLA HOFFERT

For most of my life, I have had the feeling that I was different in some way. The feeling that something must be wrong with me, that I don't fit in. I wasn't good enough. I had to prove my worth. I was always hustling; I had a work-your-ass-off mindset.

Painful childhood experiences of abuse, abandonment, deceit, molestation, and family betrayal followed me into adulthood, contributing to this way of thinking. These experiences were so heavy that carrying them rocked my mind out of balance. At one point, I even questioned the purpose of life – was it really worth it? Deep depression was the norm; suicide lingered in the back of my mind, sometimes daily. It was a dark night of my soul.

We receive the strongest social conditioning from birth to seven. As little ones, we believe these as truths, and they get locked into our mindset. They come from our environments, such as chaotic households with drugs and or alcohol misuse, and the mannerisms of caretakers, teachers, and community leaders. We can relate this to a garden as we grow. Like a plant, we begin to realize some of the earlier programming isn't necessarily fact.

Weaving: The ancient act of recognizing health and wholeness as the primary state. The overcoming of blockages of broken connections. Weavers are healers of the unbroken whole.

Gardening: The act of cultivating or tending to. It also represents fertility and is symbolic of happiness, purity, and salvation.

Spiritual Alchemy: The act of inner transformation, healing, and freeing the inner parts of ourselves that need change. This transformation helps lead us to liberation, bringing freedom from our fears and beliefs that no longer serve us. Example: Lingering old programming from our childhood years results in soul loss and other self-destructive and sabotaging behaviors and patterns that hinder our growth. In my opinion, our soul is much like a garden. We are each in control of our own unique gardens. Prior to our arrival here on this 3rd ROCK from the sun, we are given a preplanned itinerary with our assignment of what we are to work on in this lifetime. We cling to the beliefs that are going to trigger us enough to work through those things. Hence, "It is not happening *to* you. It is happening *for* you." View it as a magical twist.

Magical Twists: Triggers happen as the soul's way of getting our attention. Most of us were taught to override the triggers. Hence, our soul of the inner child. Especially as teens and sometimes as adults too. Don't cry right now, don't act that way in public, and definitely don't lash out that way.

Self-care Reminder: Gardens unattended with weeds disregarded are ever ready to choke the good, healthy plants and flowers.

Without our continuous tending with the spade and hoe, the flowers and plants will soon disappear. Practice using your self-care tools regularly as an act of Love to yourself. I like to visualize life gardens as a magical circle of kinetic energy "where you leave some room for the angels to dance." Each of our gardens contains different energies at each season, from the moment our soul is birthed on this planet. Behold, angels are present as we all have one guardian angel assigned to us from birth until the last breath is expelled from our bodies. We are never on this journey alone, and we need only ask our angels, guides, and spiritual teams for help, and they respond with an unconditional flow of Love. As the keepers of our own gardens, we are in charge. We determine what to plant, what to edit out, what weeds need pulling. We are the only ones responsible for planting the boundaries for us. Plant seeds of communication; provide nourishment, water, and fertilizer.

Womanhood Stages of Life Envisioned Through Three Garden Paths

Maiden Garden: Youthful, curious, openness, sense of adventure. It is associated with the waxing moon, the start of a new growing cycle of late winter and springtime. The maiden stage can happen multiple times in our lives; for instance, when we go back to school or learn a new skill or hobby. It signifies having excitement about life's opportunities through the channeling of spirit.

Mother Garden: This is represented by the full moon (our fullest part of life). The idea of motherhood has long been associated with safety, love, security, and home. It is sometimes portrayed as matronly and plump; however, it lives within all women regardless of maternal status. It represents the fullness of life (growing season and the start of the harvest). Early ideas and possibilities that happened with the maiden are now coming to fruition.

Crone Garden: This is represented by the waning moon (when a cycle comes to an end and a new beginning starts). The crone is full of wisdom and life experience. Superficial associations with the crone can be fear, pain, and bitterness; however, if we choose to go beyond this we will see it can represent our innate wisdom and strength. Life storms will leave their marks. The crone demonstrates how you and I can come out stronger and more resilient than ever. Trauma changes all of us; it is stored in our bellies (also known as the solar plexus (third) chakra and is yellow in color.) Trauma is also linked to traumatic childhood experiences. That being said, I would like to share one traumatic experience where, with the grace of angels, GOD, and my intuition, my life has gracefully changed. This experience occurred over a decade ago, and is an example of a Maiden Garden, stemming from ignoring big red flags, ignoring my intuition, and taking this on as a challenge.

I had entered into an abusive, toxic relationship that continued well into my Mother Garden. One morning, while having coffee, I experienced mild to severe gastrointestinal symptoms. These symptoms were not new to me. I started an elimination process of food and drink from my diet, including coffee and other potential irritants. Some improvement was shown in a couple of weeks, and I slowly reintroduced foods as I had done many times before.

Then, on another morning, while reading a newspaper at my kitchen counter, I was offered a cup of coffee that I unconsciously accepted. Halfway through, I experienced a metallic taste on my tongue, followed by convulsive-like abdominal pain that had me gripping the armrest of my chair with tears streaming down my face. Suddenly, I heard a stern voice whisper, "Go to the doctor." When I paused, the voice became louder, saying, "Call for help, NOW."

Reluctantly, I went to the ER, where medical staff ordered a CT scan with contrast. At an office visit the following day, I received what I call an angelic message from above. It was not the scan, which was inconclusive, but the statement of the GI physician at the end of the visit at which I was accompanied by a toxic male: "Are you sure it's not (toxic male) that is making you sick?"

I share this story as a reminder that domestic violence and traumatic experiences can and do change you, but it is never too late to create a new life. Steps to take include putting yourself first. Love yourself, beginning with little baby steps. Invest in you. Raise your vibration by doing things that light you up. Learn a new skill, celebrate all the small things. Join a community or club that captures your interest. Practice sacred rituals. Dance, laugh, play. I highly recommend investing in a mentor or coach and doing some energy work on and for yourself.

Did you notice that some of what I mentioned refers back to the Maiden Garden? Go ahead and give yourself permission to have those firsts I did and continue to do. If you recall a particular dream, ask yourself, "Was it a dream or a message?" I highly recommend having a dream journal beside your bed. Write down whatever you recall from a dream, whether it makes sense or not.

As mentioned, I have learned that we pick up habits from early childhood and carry them into adulthood. Eventually, we realize that these are not hard truths, just early programming that stuck to us. We are here to grow, not just sprout; we learn that not all things in life are in our best interest or highest good. We can now let go of old stagnant energy with grace and ease, allowing the energy to flow. This includes letting go of people, toxic relationships, old beliefs, et cetera that no longer serve you. The peace you'll feel without these toxic relationships is worth being the villain in their story. Walk away, keep moving, stay strong, and be your own BFF. Manage your energy. Practice anything that works for you as far as Mind, Body, and Spirit.

Taking care of our bodies is the greatest blessing we can bestow upon ourselves. Think of it as if we are allowing this to rub off onto others like rubbing a magic lamp of reflection. This is what I experienced when I started healing my inner wounds – it was a feeling and a knowing of coming back to wholeness and oneness. After the completion of lesson(s), forward movement is obtained; it is like a second chance or do-over to live your life on your terms, to regain your power and retrieve parts of your soul. I noticed many transformations taking shape like Cleopatra turning metals into gold. Through the course of reuniting with myself, I have unearthed new perceptions. It feels like a new chapter of life, a newly discovered "garden." Again, we have free will as to how we tend to that garden. Love yourself first and foremost, then allow the experiences of some firsts back into your life.

These recommendations helped me recognize where I was self-sabotaging and how I could become stronger. Have healthier relationships, friendships, peace, and a happier, less stressful lifestyle. Of course, I did not come upon all of this alone. I have always immensely battled with asking for help, but I overcame this through self-help classes and a strong desire to learn more. Most importantly, I allowed myself to invest in myself, which helped me clear my feelings of unworthiness.

I want to express gratitude to all the wild women in this book for all their kindness, guidance, and blessings. A big hug of gratefulness to my mentor, who I feel blessed to have in my life, and gratitude to all the kind souls I have met while writing this chapter. Here, I share some insights, tidbits, and affirmations that have assisted me on this journey.

"I welcome relationships that are more fulfilling and call forth those people who understand my soul."

"You can't love someone into loving you."

"You are creating more good things for yourself by being extra good to yourself."

"Self-care is also choosing not to argue with people who are committed to misunderstanding you."

"Happiness and creation are an inside job, and your abundance is spoken by your output. Input=Output."

"Put your soul on a budget. You can't afford negativity, doubt, drama, bad vibes, or hate."

"If you have been in situations that caused you a lot of grief, look at the silver lining. Maybe it's time to look at the sunrise and begin to live again."

"It's not your job to detox toxic people. It's your job to detox the part of you that resonates with their toxicity."

"I am rising from the ashes to prove to myself that I can heal, forgive, and thrive."

"Your body doesn't lie."

"Healing doesn't necessarily mean the damage never existed. It means the damage no longer needs to control your life."

Thank you for another first. I am truly honored to be part of this book and have the opportunity to be a published author.

Joyful Healings,

Karla

☾

Since Karla's first steps upon the earth, she has affectionately been fond of gardens, starting with herbs and flowers and, later, rocks and minerals. Fairies and angels have always been part of her life, including her forty-plus years of service in Western medicine. Karla is also an entrepreneur and spent more than twenty as a Licensed Massage Therapist, eventually expanding into energy work such as Reiki, Crystal Reiki healing, and emotional release with essential oils. Karla is also a Reiki Master Teacher, college massage therapy instructor, and mind, body, and soul mentor.

When she's not working, Karla loves cooking different cuisines, entertaining, and snuggling with her cat, Nakata. She also enjoys listening and dancing to some good old rock-n-roll and taking adventures in nature, including river walks. Karla believes there is an invisible power in all our experiences. If you would like to work with her on discovering the energy and power behind your own story, reach out to her at:

karla_hoffert@hotmail.com

Sink, Swim, or Bob

AMY M KOKOLES

So many times in our lives, we are told to be kind or reminded to be nice. To sugarcoat things or tread lightly so people's feelings won't get hurt. What if, as much as it does hurt, we need to hear the truth? Not the fluffy made-up truth, but the facts, whether we like them or not. Maybe we need to have the sugarcoating washed off and stomped, so hard by reality, that we finally get it. That sometimes the things we want aren't good for us. That the people who promised to love us can't love us anymore, and the commitment they made to stay forever is broken because they decide forever is too long.

When this slap of reality comes calling, it isn't kind or nice. It isn't sugary or sweet. It comes in with a sickening sour taste that ruins your taste buds, at least for a while. It stomps in with spiked heels that dig into you so deeply and cause so much pain that you know you're going to have scars forever. You're devastated, you don't understand why this is happening to you, and you swear that you'll never allow yourself to feel this horrible again.

Then, with time, the sour taste lessens, and the scars left by the spiked heels fade. You have taken a time-out and now have the confidence to jump back into life. You know there were lessons and experiences that you needed to learn, and you swear this time, you learned from them.

Then it hits you, and you feel different deep down in your soul. You realize those experiences brought about a beautiful change in you. You have a freedom that you have never felt before. And you know that everything you went through has been for your benefit.

Whether you wanted to change or not, it happened. Maybe you sought it out or, maybe, like a tidal wave, it came unexpectedly and swept you out to sea, then left you afloat in the middle of the vastness. And as you look around, you realize you are alone. There is no one coming to save you, and there is no lifeboat.

It can be easy to give up when things happen, allowing the circumstances to harden our hearts. Sometimes we pull back and isolate ourselves, deciding that's safer than engaging in life.

But it's in these difficult times that you have to make a decision: Do I sink, swim, or bob?

Growing up, I was told not to rock the boat or cause waves. To keep my mouth shut and just go with the flow. To never, ever talk about it, whatever, "it" happened to be that day. So, I did what I was told and as a family we buried our heads and our issues in the sand.

I spent so much of my childhood worrying and fearing that one day, the sand pile would come crashing down, and all that was buried would be exposed. I hated having to live this way, and it caused me to never feel truly safe. I needed to talk about the things that were happening. I wanted to have actual conversations with my family and hear their opinions. To have the ability to share my feelings and my thoughts. To count on their love and support as I tried to navigate my way through life. For them to encourage me to always be myself. And the security of knowing that no matter what, my family would never turn their backs on me. That I would always have a safe shore to call home. But that isn't how my life was.

I grew up hearing and knowing that I was "too much." No matter how I spoke, acted, or dressed, there was always an emotional undercurrent of what my family thought about me. I was told that I talked too much, and nobody wanted to hear it. That my voice was too loud and I needed to stop yelling. I was continuously reminded that I should keep what I was thinking and feeling to myself because I might hurt someone's feelings. I was accused of trying to always be the center of attention and told repeatedly that it wasn't always about me. In fact, one of my sisters said it on the day of my bridal shower.

I can laugh about that ... now.

For so many years, I was labeled and placed in a box. This box contained all the stories my family believed about me. And it held all the lies my family told about me, including the lies they told me about myself.

I knew deep inside that what they were saying about me wasn't true. I desperately wanted and needed my life to be different. But every time I tried to get out of my box, they pushed me back inside. I refused to give up and kept trying to get out, but nothing I did was working. I soon realized that instead of pushing to get out of my box, I could slowly start going through the stories and lies that were inside of it. As I started going through everything in my box, it became obvious that nothing inside was actually mine. With that realization, my box grew weaker, and I was finally able to get out of my box and break free of it forever. This breakout caused my mom and three of my four siblings to fall out of my life. To say that this was one of the most traumatic — and amazing — things that ever happened in my life would be an understatement.

I use the phrase "fell out" because it's the kindest way to say it. I was struggling to find myself, my place in the world, and my beautiful, authentic voice. The people who were supposed to love me unconditionally didn't like that I was rocking the boat. But I didn't care. I kept rocking the boat until it capsized, and we were all thrust into the ocean. That's exactly what I wanted, needed, and craved. To have things so shaken up that we were all forced to finally deal with that insurmountable pile of sand. But it backfired. I watched as my siblings and mom jumped on the only lifeboat and sailed away together.

As the reality and gravity of what I had wanted and had accomplished set in, I realized that I was all alone. I couldn't see over the immense waves that crashed against my body. The force of the water carried me back and forth, throwing me into spins that disoriented me time and again. It was then that I realized I had to make some decisions. I knew I couldn't go back to what was ever again; I made sure of that. I weighed my options and realized that I could sink by letting the waves of grief drown me. I could bob and just stay in the exact same place, being battered and disoriented by the ocean. Or I could swim. I knew in my heart that the only option I had, or wanted, was to swim.

As I started the long swim back to a new, safe shore, I started to pick apart my life. I thought about all the things I was told, about who I was and who I needed to be. I began to remember how lonely I had felt growing up, even though there was a house full of people. And the frustration and sadness I felt when I was labeled and put into my "box." I wasn't, I realized, the person my siblings and mom told me I was. I was beautiful and strong and had a right to my opinions. My voice wasn't too loud, and I enjoyed talking because I was excited by life. As I continued to dive into all the things that my family didn't like about me, I realized that they were the things that made me uniquely *me*. The deeper I went into remembering my childhood, the harder the waves would crash against me, but I kept going.

Then, one day, I realized the ocean was calm. As I looked back over my shoulder, I saw the waves that could have drowned me if I let them. As I looked forward, I saw my beautiful new safe shore and knew I was almost home. When I got to shore, I was blessed to meet a man who became my compass.

John encourages me not to bury my head or my issues in the sand. He always wants to hear me and allows me to speak what is on my heart; he's my best friend and would never leave me or stop loving me. My husband never gives up on me. When I think about sinking, he's there to encourage me to swim. On the days I feel like bobbing, he lets me know it's okay to just hang out for a while and that he's with me. John allows me to be whatever I need to be each day. He accepts all of me. When I start filling my head and heart full of old stories, he is there to make sure I know the truth.

As I look back, I can take a long, deep breath and realize that I needed my ocean journey to discover who I was. All the struggles I went through were the sparks that lit the flame that grew into the light that I am today. I stand in the beautiful soul that I am because of being left in the ocean alone.

It would be so easy for me to sit back and go over everything that happened and be sad or angry, but I'm not. I still do have minutes or days when the sadness creeps in without reason, but when I sit with myself, the reason always comes through. Each time it does, it's because something in me or in my life needs to change.

I always used to say that I hated change; I said it so many times I wore that statement to death. It wasn't until I was out there in the middle of the ocean alone that I realized I had to embrace change in order to survive.

I finally realized it's in the changing that I became more me. Happier, more genuine, more caring, and loving – not just to others, but, most importantly, to me. I can see now that every issue, tear, word, and action led me to who I always wanted to be.

I've had to say goodbye to a lot of people along the way; yes, it was painful, and I still miss them sometimes. But for me to change I had to leave some people alone in the ocean. I don't want to think about where I would be right now if I hadn't gone through the things that were put before me or if I had just decided to bob or, worse yet, sink.

Today, I can say I'm sad, and it can just be that simple. Maybe someone told me something about myself that I know isn't true. Or maybe it's that I finally decided it was time to say goodbye to a friend with whom I no longer resonate. Sometimes, as much as we want it, some people cannot go on our journey with us. And it's better to put them on the only lifeboat there is and send them off with love and well wishes.

I know the next time I am in the middle of the ocean, deciding whether it's time to sink, swim, or bob into my next big adventure, I can guarantee that I will swim.

I will embrace the changes that come from me getting through the waves crashing against my body. Every single time knowing that the changes that I am going through, the pain, sadness, and frustration will always bring me back to me. Better, wiser, and more in love with who I am and who I am allowing myself to be.

Amy M Kokoles is a Reiki Master Teacher, international best-selling author, personal development coach, speaker, mentor, teacher, and certified angel guide. After years of ignoring the whispers of her soul, Amy embarked on a spiritual journey to live as her most beautiful, authentic self.

As part of her spiritual journey and service to others, Amy created the Facebook group, "Becoming You ~ Beautiful Whispers," a sacred space that provides a nurturing and supportive environment for women to embrace their authentic, beautiful selves. In addition, she offers mentorship for personal and spiritual development, Angel card readings, and Reiki healing sessions available in person or online.

Amy has spent the last several years volunteering in her community, for which she received The President's Volunteer Service Award and has been interviewed for numerous articles and podcasts.

Amy lives in the suburbs of Philadelphia with her husband and best friend, John, and their much-loved and spoiled fur babies. To learn more about Amy and her work, visit:

amykokoles.com

Death & Co.

MAKAYLA JAMES

Every time there's a full moon or a change in the zodiac season, online astrologers and coaches start pumping out memes with powerful sounding words like "transformation," "expansion," and "rebirth." Now is a time, they say, to let go of what no longer serves you and manifest your dream life! Yeah, yeah, sounds nice and all, but if it was so easy to just "let go," wouldn't we all have done that already?

The promise of rebirth, new beginnings, and expansion certainly sounds sexy and enticing. Who doesn't want to wake up tomorrow to find themselves in a brand-new beautiful home and whatever else they desire – and all because Venus was hanging with Pluto and Saturn in their second house? I get it. The dream, hope, and promise of a better life – that's what sells.

What does *not* sell is the reality of what it takes to make a huge life change or, for that matter, even a small one. It's not easy, it's not pretty, and it's certainly not sexy … unless, of course, you have one of those cries while eating kinks. In which case, no judgment.

What no one ever talks about is that new beginnings generally come as a result of a very painful ending. In order to be reborn, you must die. Uncomfortable as it sounds, it's true. To get to the new version of self, you first have to get rid of the old, and fuck if she's not one clingy bitch.

Good news: though it is hard, it is worth it. Also, you don't have to do it alone – the dying, I mean. A team is already around you, ready to guide and support you during your transition. It's their job, and they're really good at it. You just have to reach out, accept the help, and of course, do the work. If you're lucky (and I bet you are) you'll also get major synchronicities along the way to give confirmation that you're exactly where you're supposed to be. But I'm getting ahead of myself here, so let's get back to the doom and gloom for a bit.

As someone who was recently released from Dark Night of the Soul Penitentiary, I have the inside info. If you want to change, you better mean it because this is one hell of an initiation. You will be pushed to the threshold of what you think you can tolerate, and then you'll be pushed some more. At times, you may feel as if you are going crazy and, honestly, maybe you are. You will cry, scream, and question all of humanity over and over. When you finally pick yourself up from the closet floor after having what has to be the third breakdown of the week, you'll wipe your nose with that cute embroidered towel, and you will be asked to do it all over again. And just when you think you cannot take anymore, and you feel you are literally being torn apart from the inside out, there's a crack. Just a tiny bit of light starts to slip through the opening and gives you some relief. You now have hope. That hope wipes your tears, takes your hand, and leads you right to the edge of reality. It looks at you, smiles, and waves as it pushes you right over the threshold down into the deep, dark abyss.

After my marriage of twenty-two years officially started to crumble, I found myself in quite the predicament. I had fought hard and was so proud because I won! I had gotten exactly what I had asked for. My ex-husband moved out, and the divorce proceedings began. Yay, I'm free! Oh, honey, no. It's bittersweet to look back at myself, bright-eyed and so full of hope. No one ever told me that getting what you want comes with serious consequences. Lucky me, I was about to find that out.

I had gotten so used to focusing on the goal of getting out while living in the day-to-day stress that I didn't realize how much free time I would have once it was over. It opened up a lot of space to just be with myself. Here was the problem with that: one, I didn't like myself very much; two, there was a lot of stuff I didn't want to acknowledge or deal with. This didn't feel so good. It's why chaos was awesome: it kept me distracted and busy, and if you're constantly focused "out there" you never have to stop and look at what's going on "in here." The biggest problem with looking inside is that's where all the stuff is, the bad stuff you've been carrying with you since you were young, and the additional things you've picked up since.

After my divorce was official, my mental health did not get better; it got worse. After years of holding it all together, my physical body could no longer hold all the emotional pain. My depression and anxiety left me so paralyzed that I isolated myself more and more. There wasn't a lot that would soothe me, and I found it hard to sit still. One thing that helped was taking a bath. It became my evening ritual, and the one thing I looked forward to every day. Each night, I would make my way upstairs, turn off all the lights, put some music on, and lay in the bath for what seemed like hours. It was the one place I could cry without anyone seeing me, and the one place I could close my eyes and actually feel safe to unclench my jaw for a while. Something about the darkness mixed with the sound and feel of the warm water was very soothing.

I don't know where the idea originally came from, but I also started a daily writing and somatic movement practice around the same time. The writing started out as a way to purge all my thoughts from my head and onto paper, in no structure or order. Over time, those random thoughts and feelings started to become coherent. The unstructured writing gave me the ability to explore with no motivation or expected outcome. I started digging up old memories, many of which had been forgotten, and eventually began to feel comfortable acknowledging and admitting things I had never dared to before. I also was able to connect the old traumas I uncovered with the most recent things I had been through. Understanding the whys also brought relief to my logical brain. If I could understand the why, then I could figure out the how.

The somatic exercises allowed me to release those same traumas from my physical body. These simple movements opened a door that had been locked for years. Flashbacks and deeply buried memories started pouring out almost immediately. It was scary going back to those times, and especially frightening when there was no story or visual to match what my body was feeling. I started crying a lot, and all the uncovering and processing of emotions left me extremely raw and vulnerable.

I don't sugarcoat things, but there is a part of me that wants to lie to you right now and say the bath rituals were a result of my subconscious desire to be held by my mother, and so I was recreating the womb. I would tell you in those nights I transformed, and finally, when I had fully healed, I was reborn! I would present this profound moment to you, pause dramatically for reaction, and then let fly a lot of fist-pumping and "fuck, yeahs." But that's not what it was … not at all.

I didn't know it at the time, but my very own Dark Angel was the one guiding, supporting, and holding me during the process of my death.

The parallels between an emotional death and rebirth is much like that of a physical death. My grandpa passed away five years ago, and I was there in the days leading up to his death. One night, he told my grandma, "Go get Makayla; she'll take me." When I walked back to his room, he said, "I want to go home." Assuming he thought he was in the hospital, I replied, "You are home." How I regret that! After repeating over and over, "I want to go home," he suddenly asked, "Who are all the people in the room?" I didn't know it then, but now, as a medium with more experience and training, I can say with certainty that they were his Angels of Death.

Santa Muerte, Archangel Raziel, or The Grim Reaper – these psychopomps are all feared and the names alone may conjure up horrifying images. Why is that? They aren't coming *for* you; they are coming *to* you. I can't think of anything more loving than a team of beautiful spirits coming to comfort you as you prepare and then to walk beside you when the time comes – all so you don't have to take this journey alone. How comforting to know that the people we love are fully surrounded and supported as they transform in order to leave this reality and enter another.

Because I was also surrounded by a beautiful Dark Angel as I was transforming, I was able to keep going. I was given the gift of synchronicities so powerful they could not be ignored or "coincidenced" away. I was yelling, cursing, and smashing anything and everything in my way, but the point is, I kept going. For the first time in my entire life, I kept showing up, I kept doing the work, and I was doing it all for me. Fucking hell, I even got a therapist!

After some tough years of darkness, and even praying for death, I now sit on the other side. I made it. I'm currently in Dubai because my life is amazingly abundant and I'm rich as hell because Jupiter and Venus went into Taurus and … No, not true, but you know what *is*? My life is good. Most days I feel really calm, and even if I do get anxious, there is a peace deep inside me that I have never felt before. I am finding my way, and finding out who I am now, and it's exciting. Plot twist: I even kinda like myself. So. Awkward.

When the Angel of Death comes, there is no escaping. There are many theories and ideas about what death actually is and where you go afterward – that is, if you go anywhere at all. Entire religions are built upon answering the question, "What happens when we die?"

I don't know where your death will take you or what awaits you on the other side. I can't promise that your demise will be pain-free, quick, or easy. What I can promise is that whatever you have to go through to get to your new self, it is worth every single moment.

Dying is easy. It's the living that's hard.

Water Burial Ceremony

While this ceremony is simple in form, I encourage you to make it as elaborate as possible. Plan ahead, go shopping, and set a date and time when you can have at least one or two hours to yourself, uninterrupted. This is not about manifesting or focusing on goals; this ceremony is to honor you and the life you have now that you are leaving behind.

1. **Journal** – Write about your life, the highs and lows, and what brought you to this moment. Allow all feelings to come up and be acknowledged, but don't get stuck here. The deep work will come later. Remember, you are honoring yourself, so try as best as you can to give yourself compassion and grace with the things you write. Just a page or two.

2. **Flowers** – Get as many different kinds and colors as you can. This is not about symbolism or meaning, buy them simply because you love them.

3. **Essential Oil** – Get a bottle of your favorite scent; ensure it is pure oil and not artificial. If food grade is available, get that. Watch out for peppermint or anything that would irritate the skin. It might smell nice, but peppermint makes you feel like your skin is on fire and freezing at the same time. Ask me how I know.

4. **Music** – Make a playlist of your all-time favorite songs. Songs from your childhood, teen angst days, wedding day, driving-alone music, et cetera. If you love it, add it. The only caveat: you absolutely are forbidden to add "If I Die Young" by The Band Perry.

5. **Bathtub** – You know what to do here, fill it up and add all the stuff, then turn the music on. Make it pretty!

6. **Ceremony** – When you slip into the water, feel into your body; be present with yourself. The water is a bubble of protection, a safe space. Stay here, honoring yourself for as long as you like. You deserve it.

☾

Makayla James is a dedicated medium, Reiki Master, and astrologer. Growing up, she was highly empathic and always seemed to just "know" things beyond the ordinary. Makayla was naturally drawn to stories of magical realms and all things otherworldly, and she remained hopeful that one day she would see proof those stories were real. At age seventeen, while browsing in a bookstore, she stumbled upon a book titled, *Ask Your Angels: A Practical Guide to Working with the Messengers of Heaven,* which changed the trajectory of her life.

As a medium, Makayla takes great pride in helping people connect with loved ones who have crossed over, bringing them comfort, healing, and sometimes, much-needed closure. Her approach is compassionate yet straightforward – she believes in delivering messages with honesty and clarity, not just "love and light." Whether you're seeking to connect with the Other Side, heal energetically, or understand your astrological chart, Makayla's here to assist you on your journey.

makaylajames.co

The Alchemy of Gratitude

JACQUIE LAMICA

I guess I am a wandering soul, and that feeling took hold of me as a young girl. I had a family that provided me with so much support and love! I was trusted and had lots of neighborhood girlfriends. Life was good. There were many adventures in my younger years. We would go to the coast; the beaches were amazing to me! Being near the great ocean spurred so many possibilities for travel and learning. Then there were our yearly camping trips to the giant redwoods that carried so much ancient history.

When my brothers came along, the dynamic of my life changed. I began to grow up and, unbeknownst to me, I would be an example and a caregiver to these wild and crazy boys. That was when I started writing about my dreams. I'd always had vivid dreams; it was a way to process growing up, although I was only twelve, I felt so much older. My friends in middle school seemed so much more advanced in their lifestyles, and, being a listener, even then, I became the go-between with them and their perspective boyfriends. This is where I started with a big heart, wishing to make situations and life better for them, and once again, becoming the care person for the hearts of those around me. I learned this thing called gratitude. Back in the '60s, no one talked about being grateful; it was called having manners and consideration for others.

Grace has also been a theme in my life. Grace is the way a ballerina moves across the stage as her long legs reach for the perfect toe stance; is it a beautifully plumed white swan that floats on a lake bowing her long-curved neck; it is a mother holding her newborn baby, feeling the glow of seeing true innocence and trust. I have seen it in caretakers, daughters, and sons holding their elderly parents' hands as they walked slowly from one destination to another. Children who looked up to their parents for answers and parents trying to be authentic and teach their children how to love and respect others. Grace is all around us in everyday life, so the question is, how did these people arrive at this state of grace and giving of themselves? Was it from the power of prayer or simply because someone was gracious enough to them? Were their hearts opened to receive gratitude early in their lives? There are so many stories of those who came before us, who put others before themselves. These selfless, beautiful souls have made our lives bearable when no one else could have even cared.

I learned as a young woman to listen to others; not just hear what they said but really listen to the meaning of their words. I watched their body language, saw their hearts, and listened to their concerns, then tried to uplift them so they could see some light where they thought there was only darkness and despair. I became very good at listening with my heart. I believed in gratitude, and it became very easy for me to express. When I listened to everyone else's problems, I became even more grateful that I didn't have to deal with those tribulations. I was transforming just by being present. There are many lessons in life – some bold, some very subtle – and they shaped me into the person I am now.

I knew unconditional love was the answer. I knew this because my family instilled it in me. This now became my quest and my reason for living: to show others that they were cared for and heard. This compassion also showed me many other things. It showed me I had to be careful of my own heart, it showed me that there were people out there who had no heart for anyone but themselves. People had agendas and performed tasks that made them look good, with no regard for the ones who needed compassion and love. I knew this had to change, so I became that person who studied, read many books, and sought out coaches and mentors to teach me how to bring magic back into my life.

I needed to know what was happening to me. I can truthfully say I never set out to hurt anyone, and I had never really been hurt either. I didn't know what it was like to have someone speak words to tear me down. I didn't have anyone to talk to about these experiences; no one would tell me I would be okay. I wanted to be strong, and if that meant being silent and internalizing the wrongs that I saw and experienced, so be it.

I began to write poetry again to help me through this time of tribulation. This simple act of writing down my feelings became an art form that brought me great joy. The way the words would flow, forming beautiful sentences and sentiments that others could see and relate to, became my gift. It worked for me a long time, and I was always able to find my way back to being grateful. I'm pretty sure there was a force greater than I and that angels were watching over me, protecting the fine balance of my life and maintaining my happiness.

Then I met someone and trusted in love. I was innocent; after all, I grew up with love, and I knew that by giving love, I could get love. I had to walk this path of trust, and that's where I went wrong. I had given away my power! My life was no longer magical; it became dark and uncertain. I had to look deep into my soul and face the fear of uncertainty and the unknown. I had to search in the dark places of my life, and I had to look at my shadows, even though I didn't understand what they were. I was alone again, and I couldn't find grace.

My mother was a spiritual woman and she prayed for everyone. I began to backtrack to her and the things she'd taught me and prayed for the magic to come back. I took up a new craft; it felt good, and I knew it would help others. This practice was Reiki, a hands-on approach to helping people heal but not through what we know as modern-day medicine. Reiki is a soul medicine. I learned to let go and trust in meditation and reaching for the stars where, I believed, live the answers from our elders, ancestors, or whatever resonated with you. I found a wonderful mentor who helped me hone my Reiki skills. This is when everything changed for me.

My mentor had a client, whom I'll call Mary, and she had a domesticated wolf, though I never believed you could take the wildness out of such an animal. Mary's beautiful wolf was riddled with cancerous tumors, and the vet said there was really nothing that they could do except to make him comfortable. Needless to say, Mary never left him alone. One day, I happened to be at my mentor's home when Mary came for her session. I immediately agreed when

I was asked to sit with the wolf. I knew it would help my soul and if it would make the wolf happier to have somebody with him in the absence of his master. We sat for about an hour, and since I was certified to perform Reiki I laid my hands upon him and let him know that he was loved. It was an intense feeling. I was deep into the experience, reaching for the stars, reaching for ancestors, reaching for a source to show me the path to creating health. It was a life experience I will always treasure, though it scared me as well. I felt different and even had hope I had made his life better and brought me happiness.

A month later, Mary returned, saying she wanted to thank me for what I did for her companion. It turns out that I had healed the wolf! The same specialists who had said they could not do anything about the tumors in his body were astounded when they saw his latest X-rays. There was no sign of the cancer or any sickness that had been there before. The wolf would live a long life. I couldn't believe it, and at the same time, some part of me was apprehensive. Where did the cancer go? Had it passed from his body through mine, or was it stuck in mine now? Did I manifest his cancer? That's when I gave up Reiki and asked for answers.

I guess we are always looking for those answers. There are so many facets to our growing and evolving self-awareness. I had to get real with what I wanted for the rest of my life. This is where I will insert that I am in my golden years; yep, twenty-eight more years, and I will be a centenarian!

I have heard people say that I have plenty of time to live a full life. It's never too late! I have always been a student, always reaching for more knowledge and skills so I can achieve happiness and peace.

The truth is, I am happy with my life and grateful to have grand-children whom I love and adore. While practicing gratitude – and yes, we all must practice it – I began to align myself with like-minded people who showed me that I, too, was clearly understood and heard. Kindness and gratitude became my normal. I slowed down and stopped overthinking, and stopped comparing my life to others. Every day I wake up and list five things I am grateful for and allow this to propel my day; then, I can cope better with whatever comes my way.

Do you see why I believe alchemy is magical? It is not giving up when adversity shows up; it is knowing there is more behind what is presented to us. Looking for the good, whether it be in another person or a situation we are currently dealing with. Alchemy is giv-ing without expectation, not knowing the result, being and acting with kindness. Synchronicity plays a big role; behind the scenes, some things just line up and work toward the best outcome. The simple act of paying it forward helps us realize that we are grateful for the things we have and can share with those who do not have the same. I leave with you my story of transformation and self-dis-covery. I am not always spot-on, but I do practice the art of gratitude and being kind as much as I can. My words and my story were meant to share with you, my reader, a glimpse into what works for me at this point in my life. Remember, these are my golden years, a time of reflection, a time to see the beauty of what love and magic have provided for me thus far. I leave this for you to ponder: be kind, spread love, and be grateful for what you have, as it is all the little things that make a difference. You are the magician of your life, and the wand you wield is a true source of hope and dreams, so carry on, friend, and make them come true.

☾

Jacquie Lamica is a lifelong writer who loves using words to manifest peace and happiness. Jacquie has been published in three compilation books and has written numerous poems; she hopes to one day write children's stories as well. She is also an accomplished fiber arts designer and loves to work with her hands, creating beautiful, crocheted items. "Give me a hook and some thread, and I am happy," she is fond of saying. She has a passion for reading and loves to find the right story and get lost in the chapters of romance and fantasy. Biographies and learning about others also give her great joy. Jacquie enjoys close relationships with her four grown children, all of whom live close to her in Northern California, and her five grandchildren.

Sweet Surrender

JENNE LURA

I didn't want him at first. He was just supposed to be a foster dog that needed a place to stay until his forever home was found. Considered "damaged goods" because of the hereditary umbilical hernia he was born with, the eight- to ten-week-old Rottweiler puppy had been dumped at the vet by a heartless breeder to be euthanized. Instead, the hernia was fixed without surgery, and, in my eyes, he grew to be the most amazing creature.

Let me introduce you to the love and passion I found in Sampson and how he changed my life.

I was pretty terrified of owning him, not because of his breed, necessarily, but knowing all the obstacles we would face moving forward. He was already thirty pounds when I got him and I had no idea how much bigger he would get. For his safety, he needed to be obedient, so once I realized that he wasn't going anywhere, my heart immediately softened and I gave in. Training started immediately.

You might be surprised to learn that Rottweilers are an incredible breed. They get a bad rap, but it's from people who aren't educated or interested in being educated about them. They come from

Rottweil, Germany and were also used by the Romans as cart dogs and for protection. They are wonderful family dogs, strong in mind and body. Yes, they can look intimidating and act that way toward the wrong people, but, in my opinion, you want that! They will protect their family, home, and surroundings like no other. I know I had never felt so safe as when Sampson was around.

I had so many doubts about whether I could do a good job. Was I going to be a good owner? Could I give him the life and love he deserved? He had already been passed around to three or four homes before landing in my lap. The sheer sadness and gloom in his eyes whenever we got in the car, like he didn't know where he was going next, was heartbreaking. I felt I needed to do the best I could to make it all up to him and prove to him that he was loved, wanted, and special.

Once he realized he was stable and not going anywhere, Sampson's personality really popped out! He was so silly, sweet, and so insanely smart! (I'd only met one other dog smarter – an Australian Shepherd named Sandy.) Sampson learned how to hold down the automatic waterer and would hold it down for his Basset Hound brother, Brody, who wasn't as "street smart." (I always joked Brody got by on his good looks!) Sampson also seemed to understand how the world was supposed to work intuitively. He knew when people were good or up to no good. He was very well-socialized because I was determined to make sure he had a beautiful life.

He was around eight months old by the time he learned to walk well on the leash with no tugging. He then learned how to run alongside the bike. (I think I was a little crazy, brave, and very determined.) Commands were a must as well. He learned how to sit, shake, and speak. He also understood tricks not only in English and Spanish but also in using hand commands. That last one is not so odd when you consider that animals don't "speak" to each other so much as they use motion and body language.

His favorite things were adventures, the beach, and his girl-friend, Una. We were living in Florida at the time, and he loved going to the dog park, Fort Desoto Beach, and lying out by the lake watching the ducks. I would take five dogs down to the beach and spend hours there while we all got exercise, fun, and sun. Best office job ever. I'm a different kind of crazy. We did this three or four days a week, and I would take different dogs on different days. Sampson learned how to operate the boogie board on his own too. One day at the beach, he approached some woman on a paddle board and decided he was going to get up with her. She was so good about it. He had never been on a paddle board before.

Sampson went anywhere I could get him in – Home Depot, to go pay bills; he even dabbled in Pet Therapy work. Pet Therapy work is where you train your pet to go into places where they can be pet and socialize more with people. When we went into the hospital, Sampson took his job very seriously. He loved meeting new people and showing off his talents. He could sing on command too. I looked nuts driving down the road with five dogs in the car, windows down, and every one of them singing or howling. They were excited to go to the beach!

During one trip to Home Depot, a gentleman was very scared to approach him; he even made a comment along the lines of, "How do you dare leave the house with him?" When I explained that

Sampson was a Pet Therapy dog and did volunteer work in the hospitals, et cetera, the man approached him and petted him.

"Wow!" he exclaimed, "he's just like a normal dog!"

That comment shocked me more than anything. Of course, Sampson was a normal dog; someone had even called him an "ambassador of the breed!" But at that moment, I realized not everyone knew that.

Sampson had changed my outlook – not just of his breed, but how to be more patient, caring, and loving when needed.

One year, we (when I say "we," I mean me and the dogs) traveled from St. Petersburg, Florida, to Fargo, North Dakota. Along the way, we stopped in the Nashville area for a day or two, staying at a horse-boarding farm instead of a hotel so the kids could run around and have some freedom. Sampson had the best night when the lady we stayed with hung out with me on the porch, drinking wine and watching the sun go down. Sampson was SO happy lying in the yard, watching, smelling, and listening to all the new surroundings. Much different from apartment life. I loved watching him experience that.

We got invited to New Port Richey, Florida, one year to do an educational class for a school. The kids were learning about animals and what career they'd be interested in going into. I taught them ... Sampson taught them ... how to do nails, give him a proper bath and a good blowout, and clean his ears. They even painted his nails. I don't think any two of them were the same color. He loved getting all that attention! He liked kids, as well as any other kind of animal, as long as it was calm. He didn't like any craziness going on. He would growl to calm everyone down but, again, that was sometimes misunderstood by people. Archie, a Jenday Conure, even came along on that day. Sampson's entire life was spent surrounded by kitties too.

His sister, another Basset Hound named Maggie, raised him and taught him valuable lessons. When she passed he took it so hard. I had put him in a daycare so he could have fun while I put her down. He came home, knowing she wasn't there, and let out a go-dawful howl. Animals just know. They know before we do when something isn't right. I learned that from him too – how to watch and pay attention to his behavior.

Sampson helped me through so many hard times when I lost pets – making me get up and walk or do something to get out of the house when I really didn't want to.

He found and dug out an animal skull from a river in Minnesota. I had it tested at a local school and was confirmed to be the skull of a bison, between two hundred fifty and five hundred years old. I still have it to this day.

Sampson made me want to learn everything about dogs. Every time I dog-sat or came across a breed I didn't know much about, I would google them, trying to figure out what made them "tick." I wanted to know what actions and behaviors made them, them.

Understanding the breed you're dealing with gives you a fantastic head start in figuring out how to approach or train them properly. Most dogs want to be obedient and people-please, but some breeds – huskies, for example – prefer a "partner" situation (meaning they don't really want to be told what to do.) This extensive research prepared me for greater things. I now own a dog grooming business, and my research prepared me to look for and recognize certain behaviors – good or bad. Sampson had unknowingly altered the trajectory of my life. I quit drinking so I could be more responsible for him. I exercised more so I could keep him happy. I trained him daily because I secretly like a challenge and figuring dogs out. He challenged me. He tested me. He loved me.

Sampson made me want to change everything for him. The first few times I tried to trim his nails, two people were needed to hold him down. Later, with more patience and training, he would give me his paw. He wasn't a fan of the bath, but he loved the dryer. I would bathe him at home and then towel him dry before finishing with the hairdryer. I would do one side and say, "Okay, turn," and he'd give me a quarter turn until he'd turned all the way around and was basically dry. Imagine a one-hundred-and-fifteen-pound Rottweiler who loved his mani/pedis!

I owe everything to that dog. I wanted to be a better person, a better owner, and a better leader. Sampson gave me all of that. When he passed in 2019, I got a tattoo with his name and "You will walk with me forever" down my leg. His ashes were included in the ink. It's been five years, and I'm just now getting to the point where I can talk about him and smile with such fond memories. Sometimes a memory rolls down my cheek, but that bond and love was so strong and powerful. Some people might not get this, but I don't believe any other loss in my future will affect me the way his did. He was there every day, protecting, listening, and playing with me. The pure sight of him melted away every single stress or issue I had – instantly. I'm so sad for the people who never got to meet him. Everyone he met just loved him and was so impressed with him.

Anyone or anything that can change your life like that has a powerful soul. I don't have children, so Sampson truly was my pride and joy. This beautiful creature that no one wanted suddenly became my focus; he received all my hope, love, determination, discipline, and patience. He also sparked change within me ... and it showed. I wanted to be everything he didn't get from the beginning. He inspired me to learn dog behavior, how to master the "walk," and even to become a groomer. My grooming salon is very different from other salons. I only work on one dog at a time – no kennels or cages – which is much more comfortable for them.

How could something I didn't want become the change I didn't know I needed?

No number of chapters or books I write could ever be enough to express my gratitude toward him.

Until we're together again, I love and miss you so much, Dumplin'.

☾

Jenne Lura has a lifelong fascination with wildlife of all kinds. Born and raised near a beautiful nature conservancy in the Fargo, North Dakota area, she woke up every morning to around fifty deer in her yard. In school, Jenne excelled in choir and Spanish, and upon graduating, she traveled to Mexico with her classmates. Her deepest passions have always included animals, nature, traveling, and enhancing her sensory abilities. Jenne was once a licensed massage therapist (certified in canine massage) and enjoys aroma therapy. Her guilty pleasures include trying ice cream wherever it can be found.

Anointing the Rose:
A Journey of Self-Reverence
and Creative Alchemy

LUCINDA RAE

Over the last two decades, I've walked through the fire as a mother — facing profound challenges, and dark nights of the soul within a former family constellation. My spiritual journey during this time felt like being forged in the depths — navigating toxic patterns, manipulation, alienation from my now-adult sons, and deep loss.

Yet I've emerged from those depths each time to rediscover my joy, my passion for being a heart-centered human, and knowing inner contentment as the loving mother I am.

I don't want to dwell on those other painful details, as that's a story for another book (or maybe best to leave them in the ashes on the ground as my Phoenix tail propels me forward). However, it's important to acknowledge as we dive into this: our lived experiences can sometimes feel like a stark contradiction to the Instagram-pretty highlights reel we often see portrayed.

Despite the murky waters many of us walk through in this shared human experience, we all get the opportunity to learn how to triumph over suffering, even when we feel like giving up. Stick with me though; it gets better. The lotus knows how to push through the sludge.

It was navigating my deep-sea journey that allowed me to re-emerge, like a wide-eyed mermaid, and reconnect with the immense love at my core — that innocent sense of wonder I had as a child seeing the world through a rose-tinted lens.

Because, let's be real, we all need those moments to pause, stop and smell the roses, and simply be present in the current moment.

The natural world – roses in particular – have been a salvation when life felt like a bed of thorns. Sticking my nose into their petaled beauty like a drunken bumblebee, inhaling with my whole being — that was transcendence, however brief an escape from the mind's unruliness.

Recently, I've started playing again with the petals and plants in my own yard, rediscovering the black sage — its scent that evokes a rootedness like a beloved matriarch I knew as a child on five acres of Oregon woods and pasture; the days that were as simple as making sun-brewed tea with those fuzzy sage leaves. Inhaling a scent can be like stepping into a time machine; it takes me back to the little green witchling I was then, concocting potions with rich mud, fir needles, bits of web and feather, and specific sticky plants, making healing concoctions to share with my forest and angel friends.

I was an innate alchemist, transforming earth ingredients into magic.

It can also bring us to the depth of present oneness and that JUST IS-ness that the gift of creation can offer us. These days, I'm not that much different from that little mud pie-making, fairy-whispering kid. I harvest lilacs for pastries and tonics, collect rose petals to prayerfully blend into anointing oils for myself, and adorn my oil paintings. These awakening flower essences get infused with blessings as I root into my physical being.

My prayers mingle with the blossoms, bringing me back into my body as I play with the combinations and recipes I make.

The other day, I caught myself saying out loud — "How can I simply devote my life to the flowers?" That is filled with gratitude I am for the beauty they bring and the ease and simplicity with which they open to the light of the sun.

And so many creatives I know are here to alchemize beauty like the flowers do. Years ago in meditation, I realized my path was to embody or express divine beauty in the ways it spoke or danced through me.

I've learned to do this in various ways, through vivid abstract art accented with shimmering gold, the archetypes of the divine feminine, and motherhood through portrait abstract expressionism.

Through my Prosperity Branding Process, I midwife my clients' soul essences into visual form for their brands and websites. This involves working with archetypal energies, helping clients identify their primary archetype, along with their second and third archetypes that together express their core values and vision.

Astonishingly, around 95% of my clients resonate with the Alchemist as one of their top three archetypes. We then use this in combination to express their transformational values through visuals, messaging, social media content, and their entire online brand blueprint. They are truly weaving the principles of alchemy and metamorphosis into their businesses.

Whether they are therapists or coaches, artists or spiritual entrepreneurs, their offerings often hold space for people to transmute darkness into light, coal into diamonds. We've walked through the briars and understand that the depths can hold great value – that's where the real work happens before emerging into radiance.

This is because they highly value, like I do, the core value: TRANSFORMATION.

The very breath of alchemy itself.

For clients embodying this archetype, their brand voice and visuals evoke a sense of profound transformation, rebirth, and distillation of essence.

On the spiritual side, the messaging has a mythical, ceremonial quality that beckons the audience into an initiatory experience – descending into metaphoric underworlds to reshape reality from a primordial state. The language is poetic yet potent, inviting you to "Transform lead into gold," "Birth your highest self," and "Enter the sacred crucible" of the soul's journey.

Visuals can be rich with archetypal imagery that feels anciently sacred yet modern — elemental symbols like geometries, metallic gold, or other expressions of luminosity illustrating that transformation is happening.

On the more secular side, the voice is boldly aspirational around self-directed reinvention and unlocking your ultimate potential. You might use empowering phrases like, "Elevate your mindset/body/business" and "Upgrade your reality to the next level."

Visually, it has a modern, high-performance look with electric colors, strong geometric lines, and patterns that convey futuristic transformation.

Whether spiritual or mainstream, Alchemist brands envelop you in the energy of sacred metamorphosis. The aesthetic is dramatic yet grounded, allowing you to experientially melt down your raw self into a new iteration. It's like beholding pure energy that catalyzes personal alchemy.

This deeper work and love for archetypes has emerged from my own essence exploration. I'm intimately familiar with descending into inquiry realms and re-emerging with greater clarity, integrity, and wisdom.

The trauma we can go through as women or mothers, or just human beings still carrying our inner child, can be an ego-demolishing dark night of the soul. An endless cycle of loss and stripping away of everything you thought you were.

Yet that total surrender allowed me to personally alchemize the darkness, rebirthing again and again into a more realized version of my essential self.

With each new incarnation, I reclaimed the innocent, nature-connected child I'd been, along with a soul's ever-expanding compassion as life hurls its mudballs.

Now I wear the depth life has carved with humbling valor — a badge of endurance and authenticity earned through the fires. From a higher view, I can sometimes glimpse that mountaintop view as I appreciate the range of experiences, even sometimes extremely challenging, as a crucible for our growth and emergence as radiant essence.

This is the great magnum opus of the Alchemist's transformational path.

I continue to acknowledge the thorns that cracked me open, applying balm when there are scars, and allowing me to bloom again rose-like with each reinvention.

This desire to continually unfurl is a central theme in my life's creative process, as it is for so many on the mystical path.

Just as I guide branding clients to visually embody their essence through archetypes, I've returned to concocting botanical blends like the child I was – praying into them as allies for our flames of ego-death and resurrection.

In the ancient Hebrew Bible, anointing with sacred oil blends held deep spiritual significance. When applied, the oils symbolized the very presence and power of God's Spirit, flowing down from the heavens to consecrate and initiate the recipient. Back then, these holy oils could only be blended and utilized by the high priests; they held the exclusive responsibility for anointing people, objects, and spaces, which then allowed God's divine essence to be channeled into the material realm.

Now we get to have a direct connection with the Divine and anoint ourselves, thereby reclaiming our identity as a holy, rose-like being worthy of reverence and self-blessing. I am reinvigorating this practice for myself after so many years of desiring to leave my body, leave the ego, and transcend my spirit via meditation. Being intimately present with the senses feels like the next step of my spiritual journey – self-care and inquiry through the somatic experience.

I've been creating blends that honor the ancient ways by using resins like frankincense and myrrh, alongside other sacred botanical oils used for millennia that we get to create in self-ritual. This grounds me in deep meaning as I dot and glide the rich elixirs over my skin, allowing the warmth and intoxicating scents to awaken my divine feminine essence through embodied ritual reverence, filling me with beauty, healing, and wholeness.

In an anointed state, I move to the canvas with oil paint, allowing the oils' powerful vibrations of the botanical essences to intermingle with my brushstrokes and color and textures of the paints, infusing the art also with their ceremonial energies.

I've found in nature to others navigating paths of reinvention, awakening, trauma recovery, or simply longing for deeper self-acceptance. These prayer offerings can serve as ritualistic allies for the journey.

At the core of all my artistic and entrepreneurial work is a driving mission to alchemize pain into power, darkness into light. Whether through my abstract paintings emerging from grief or ecstatic love, my branding work helping lightworkers embody their archetypes in their online business and website, or my Anointed Rose offerings, I realize this soul's purpose seems to be creative alchemy first and foremost – midwifing beauty and illumination from the most challenging human experiences.

I invite us all to discover this truth by activating the sparkling breadcrumbs leading us on the path of our lives. To create is to engage in the highest alchemy – giving material form to the immaterial essence of our being before this body returns to Source.

Our creations extend and allow our deepest energies and essences to live on eternally. Creating is an act of magic – transforming the impermanence of human experience into enduring expressions of our passions.

We create to transmute the essence of our being into offerings that outlive us, etching the luminous frequencies of our souls into existence. Each manifestation extends our inner truth outward to enrich the shared experience long after our bodies are gone. To create is to render the immaterial into material form, the finite into the infinite... the highest alchemy we can endeavor as transcendent yet temporary beings.

We're driven by that primordial urge to leave an uplifting mark upon our fleeting existence. When brushstrokes immortalize color and lifeforce on canvas, it defies death itself – a sensual human prayer of awe before the Great Mystery.

Our creations contain the passion poured into them, allowing others to intimately experience deeper facets of ourselves made tangible. They echo our life's energies forward, ensuring our journeys and perspectives get woven into the cosmic tapestry for generations.

While this earthly life is fleeting, our conscious creations transcend limits. We imprint unique aspects of our energy into them that refract outward in kaleidoscopic prisms across the multiverse. Creating allows us to embrace our temporary existence while extending tendrils into the great continuum.

We breathe life into form through whatever medium calls to our soul's expression. It is this sacred alchemy that transforms the raw materials of our finite lives into transcendent offerings to live on infinitely.

These emanations become ceremonial beacons anchoring our soul's essence into material existence beyond this incarnation. Infused with prayers and intentions, they catalyze opportunities for metamorphosis; first for ourselves, then for all who experience them.

Each creation contains codes for our spiritual rebirth and emergence. They are symbolic essences made manifest like elixirs by which we transmute the lead experiences of our lives into inner peace.

I've dreamed these creations into being through the fires of my own becoming. As I continually refine and rebirth in new permutations of myself, so too do my offerings serve as alchemical catalysts for those who receive their transmission.

Whether through visionary art, writings, or ceremonial tools, my aim is to share the essence: our biggest pains, when lovingly met, can transmute into powerful portals of liberation.

With transformation, we reclaim the innocent essence of the child – that wild one joyfully creating magic in the forest, fully one with nature's beauty and oneness. While my offerings now contain deeper, intentional rituals, at their core shines that same wide-eyed awe and contentment in simply being. In this way, they embody the primal wonder we all felt as children before life's miraculous unveiling. A reminder to look upon our world again through those sacred beginner's eyes.

And, in this place, we can remain curious about all we've transformed with in life's wild carousel ride of ever-shapeshifting alchemy.

Anointed Rose Ritual for Self-Reverence

What you can gather:

- Anointed Rose Anointing Oil or Body Oil

- A quiet, sacred space

- A candle

- A rose or rose petals (optional)

Gentle instruction:

1. Create a sacred space by lighting a candle and placing out any rose elements. Take a few deep breaths to center yourself.

2. Hold the Anointed Rose bottle (or a blend of your choice) in your hands and tune into its energy. State your intention to use this oil for self-anointing and reverence.

3. Open the bottle and inhale the aroma deeply. Notice how the floral, herbal scents make you feel.

4. Use your finger to apply a drop of oil to your third eye point between the brows. Speak aloud: "I anoint myself with the radiance of my soul."

5. Apply oil to your pulse points – wrists, behind the ears, base of throat. Speak: "I revere the life force flowing through me."

6. If using a body oil, massage it over your heart center, belly, and soles of feet while affirming: "I honor the Divine Light within my body and being."

7. Take a few more deep breaths with the oil anointed, feeling into any energetic shifts. Visualize yourself as an exquisite rose, fully unfurled and radiant.

8. When ready, conclude by joining your palms together in a prayer pose and bowing to the beauty of your honored, integrated self.

Let this simple ritual awaken a sense of gentle adoration, reverence, and remembrance of your wholeness as you alchemize through life's journey.

Anoint yourself again whenever you need to restore connection to your essential rose-like nature.

☾

Lucinda Rae is a visionary creative and entrepreneur blazing the way for women to shine their brightest. She's the founder and CEO of Prosperity Branding, a boutique brand agency, and the author of the best-selling book *Holy Hot Visibility: Shine Brighter with Less Fear.*

As a branding expert and marketing mentor, Lucinda empowers women online business leaders to create sustainable prosperity and lasting impact through boldly expressing their authentic selves in their websites, brand visibility, and expression. Her intuitive, creative approach integrates strategic marketing with soulful sparkle.

Raised in the cosmic forested countryside of western Oregon,

Lucinda communed with nature spirits and the Divine Creator from a young age. Art became her bridge between realms, co-creating with these unseen creative forces. For over twenty years as a visual brand designer, she has infused this soulful, alchemical approach into building transformative brands.

When not empowering entrepreneurs she loves painting, playing with her apothecary, sipping abundant matcha oat milk lattes, and forest-bathing in Portland where she lives with her husband and young son. Come discover Lucinda's offerings at:

hellolucinda.com

Culinary Alchemy

GG RUSH

"It was very pleasant to savor its aroma, for smells have the power to evoke the past, bringing back sounds and even other smells that have no match in the present."

~ Laura Esquivel, *Like Water for Chocolate*

The kitchen is the heart of the home. This is my belief, and many of my memories have been made in that sacred room. I grew up with two very different grandmothers. My dad's mother, Emma, was German and lived in Ohio. She was my caregiver when I was a child, as both my parents worked, and we spent a lot of time in the kitchen. My grandmother was a fabulous cook and baker, and she made Easter and Christmas dinners served around a big table surrounded by family. I remember the big cast iron pots full of savory chicken and dumplings, German potato salad, and beautifully roasted meats, but what I loved most were her pies. The butterscotch pie was my favorite, and she taught me the art of patience when it came to stirring the simmering butterscotch, and how to whip egg whites into the frothy meringue topping.

I can easily imagine the creamy, sweet deliciousness of that pie, but I've only successfully created it once in my life. Mine always comes out lumpy or grainy, so maybe I have yet to master that art of patience when stirring.

My mother's mother, Nellie, lived on the family farm in South Carolina. I spent every summer vacation there, barefoot and content, helping to gather fresh eggs and feed the chickens and pigs. Grandma Nellie and my Great Aunt Daisy spent most of their days in the enormous kitchen, cooking from sunup to sundown. Every morning, I would wake up to the smell of Grandma's cheese biscuits. There were homemade jams and molasses to accompany them, plus fresh eggs and sausage, all from the farm.

Dinner was fried chicken, fresh green beans, deviled eggs, and cornbread, all served in big bowls on mismatched china. Aunt Daisy was a cake baker. Her cakes were legendary. We also had hand-churned ice cream, though we were the ones churning it, and not from an electric device either. At night, my mother would eat the leftover cornbread in a tall glass of milk – a special treat she still enjoys at ninety-six years old.

Memories of the kitchen were created early in my life. The aromas, the tastes and, most importantly, the love. Love was and is the secret ingredient to what I call "Culinary Alchemy."

Culinary Alchemy is the science of ingredients, herbs and spices, and a recipe that you tweak over and over to make your own. You put your heart into it to make it with love. Alchemy utilizes the four elements – Water, Fire, Air, and Earth – all of which are used in cooking. Water for boiling, diluting, blanching, and steaming.

Fire for cooking and roasting. Air is used as a temperature for heating or cooling ingredients. Now, it can be used in convection ovens and air fryers. And finally, Earth, where the ingredients – meats, vegetables, herbs and spices – are born. We can even imagine that chef donning a toque, the traditional chef's hat, and a coat or apron as a symbol of a chemist or magician – an Alchemist, if you will. The tools, pots, and pans are like cauldrons; the spoons and spatulas are wands. The combination of the elements produce the finish to the recipe. Culinary magic.

Minerals such as the much-needed salt, along with herbs and spices, are the Earth elements that flavor our culinary creations. Let us talk first about the difference between an herb and a spice. Herbs are the fresh leaves of the plant. Sage, thyme, curry, and oregano leaves are all part of my favorite spice profiles. There are so many herbal options available to the modern cook or chef. Every year I have a small herb garden that I plant and use in my cooking. My current garden has all of the above, plus catnip. Yes, I love to grow fresh catnip that I dry for my middle-aged kitty, Bella! She doesn't seem to care that it's not the usual packed herb she gets at other times of the year, but I feel like I accomplished something by growing it fresh. These days, you can find lots of options to grow in a herb garden at your local garden center. You can have a simple container garden grown on your porch or balcony, or you can dedicate an entire patch in your yard for a kitchen garden.

If variety is the "spice of life," then spice is the variety of flavor in your food. Spices come from the dried root or seed of the herb plant. Spices have the full flavor profile of the plant and are much stronger than the herbaceous part of the plant. It is so interesting to learn the distinctions. Pepper is a great example of this because it comes from the flowering vine and the peppercorns, which are ground into what we recognize as a hot spice that adds flavor to dishes. I personally love pepper.

Now, let's talk about curry, which I believe is a great example of Culinary Alchemy. There are curry leaves and curry powder, which are two very different things. Curry leaves are indeed the actual leaves of a curry plant and are used in some places as a cure for indigestion. However, curry spice – of which there are several forms – is a blended powder. My go-to curry powder is a Madras curry, a very traditional blend of coriander, cumin, fennel, turmeric, cardamom, black pepper, cloves, and a little chili, which are ground together to give us a curry powder.

There are so many different ways to incorporate herbs and spices into our Culinary Alchemy. For instance, do you use any herbs or spices on a regular basis? In chicken dishes, I like to add rosemary and thyme. Herbs de Provance, rosemary, thyme oregano, marjoram, and lavender are a staple in my Thanksgiving turkey and Easter lamb dishes. I love fresh sage in the mushroom pizza that I am still perfecting. Salt may be a "bad guy" ingredient, but it brings out the flavor of any dish you make. Try to experiment with flavors via herbs and spices. You will not be sorry.

How about oils and vinegars? In my area, there are many successful businesses that specialize in oils and vinegars. I discovered the amazing use of good olive oil and good balsamic vinegar early in my culinary journey. For instance, I only use a good grade of olive oil to start any dish – unless it is a stir-fry or Asian dish, in which case I use a good sesame oil. When making a spicy dish I use hot chili oil. Have you ever caramelized onions? They are a must for me in lots of dishes, including my go-to homemade French onion soup. I just need some olive oil and a good balsamic with some sugar for the caramelization process to make that dish taste amazing.

So far, we've covered herbs, spices, minerals, oils, vinegars, other ingredients, and recipes. But I truly believe that the real "secret" ingredient to any culinary creation is LOVE. When you step into your kitchen with the plan to make or bake a dish for your family, you have love in your heart. One of my favorite books, Like Water for Chocolate, is about just that. The main character, Tita, cried into the batter she made, literally pouring her love and soul into that recipe. To this day, my daughters still say the line from the movie "It's Made with Love" when we eat or cook. Many other favorite books, movies, and TV shows are culinary-based as well, like Eat, Pray Love by Elizabeth Gilbert, and Chef with Jon Favreau; I watch Top Chef and Gordon Ramsey shows to hone my cooking skills. Just yesterday I made that mushroom pizza based on a creation from another show, Ciao House. Did I nail it? Not exactly, but I created the basis for a dish I will continue to make until it becomes my own.

Are you a "Top Chef" or a magician? Culinary Alchemy doesn't require you to be a James Beard award winner or an institute-trained graduate. It requires you to have a passion for cooking, a love of flavor, and a little bravery.

Gordon Ramsey says, "Cooking is about passion, so it might look temperamental in a way that's it's too assertive to the naked eye." So yes, it's not visible to the naked eye, though I hear often that eating does start with the visual. What looks good should taste good, but that is not always the case. We do not actually "eat with our eyes." We eat with our noses, our tastebuds, and our hearts. And we cook with our noses, our tastebuds, and our hearts.

Now, let's cook! I am sharing one of my favorite recipes – a sweet curry dish, like a Massaman curry, that I concocted. This one has tofu for everyone, but you can substitute beef or chicken. I make mine in the "Instant Pot" because it really infuses the flavor, but you can make it on the stovetop!

Tofu Curry

1 package of soft tofu cut into pieces.

Mirepoix (celery, onion and carrots diced)

1 potato diced.

1 jar yellow curry sauce (I like Trader Joe's)

1 can of coconut milk

1 can coconut cream

1 cup of chicken stock or veg stock

1 cup jasmine rice

In a pot, sauté the mirepoix and potato in olive oil until it softens.

Add tofu. Add the jar of curry sauce. Add coconut milk and coconut cream. Add the cup of stock. Sprinkle with a "generous" helping of Madras curry powder.

Add rice.

Seal instant pot and cook under pressure for 12-15 minutes. Allow for natural pressure release.

Scoop into bowls and serve with love!

If you make this stove top, make the rice separately by melting some butter in a pot; then add your rice and allow it to cook for a minute, before adding stock or water. Serve your curry over the rice.

You can try this recipe a few times and, again, tweak it to make it yours. I like my curry spicy and sweet, so this comes out both depending on whether you use coconut cream and the amount of curry powder you use.

Today, I challenge you to schedule a field trip to a local farmers' market or garden center. Check out the herbs and really give them a good smell. Mint, lemon, and sage are great to try out your culinary nose. Look around your area for an olive oil and vinegar shop. I am sure you can locate one as they are so popular. Check out a local Asian or Indian grocery store. You don't need to break the bank, but you can start with a few choices to get started. Go to the bookstore and look at cookbooks, especially by local chefs that use local ingredients. Make an old favorite recipe, but try to spice it up and make it shine.

In the end, all it really takes is courage and love to make Culinary Alchemy. We all need to stretch our wings and go out of our comfort zones when it comes to herbs and spices. Delve into something new and exciting. Keep your senses open. Try local cuisine and restaurants. Take a class online or in person. Variety IS the spice of life. Live the Alchemy that is food and enjoy your senses!

☾

GG Rush (aka Gail Rush Gould) is an author, certified life coach, clutter-clearing coach, and clinical hypnotherapist. She is also a Reiki Master and has studied aromatherapy, chakra balancing, toxic emotions, and the ancient art of pulse reading. She has traveled the world solo and will continue her journey to see the world and find herself. GG resides in Cary, North Carolina, with her cat Bella. Learn more about her work at:

sacredsparrowspiritual.com

Manifesting Motherhood:
The Path of Positive
Intention Conception

SARA RECTOR, LMFT

D r. Carl Jung incorporated the concept of alchemy as a metaphor for psychological transformation into the process of becoming who we are meant to be in our entirety. One of the most transformational processes a woman experiences is metamorphosizing from a maiden to a mother. For most women, the desire to be a mother is compelling, beginning at an early age when she is gifted a baby doll.

Most animal behavior is designed to facilitate reproduction. The red circular area around the female Mandrill baboon's posterior acts like an attractive bull's-eye for potential mates. Red lipstick draws male attention to our lips as well. It is no coincidence, then, that the percentage of women experiencing infertility has mirrored the upward climb of women achieving financial and career success. Present-day wild women can have difficulty conceiving due to societal pressure to have it all. In delaying childbearing until we reach professional milestones, we are disregarding and denying our animal nature. We are choosing to pray to the Promethean God of progress instead of paying homage to the Goddess of Motherhood, Demeter. This sacrifices the Anima energy to feed Animus's fire, creating an internal and external imbalance.

As a Licensed Marriage Family Therapist in private practice specializing in Infertility and Family Building for the last two decades, I have counseled hundreds of women who were struggling with infertility. They come to me devastated by their inability to transition to their next life stage. After spending years using contraception to impede the biological alchemy that produces a child, they experience the reality of not being able to control the timing of what they assumed was their birthright: the ability to become a mother.

As a young woman, I, too, believed the myth that I could have it all. I decided I wouldn't marry until I was thirty because I wanted to have as much freedom and fun as possible before adulting. Fate had other plans, however; I met the love of my life and was married to him at twenty-six. My nephew was born two years later, igniting my desire for a child. It was like a biological light switch was turned on. My husband and I encountered many roadblocks on our path to becoming parents. The major one was my career, where I traveled out of town fifty percent of the time. I began to realize that my job was not conducive to being a mother. This was concurrent with a feeling of emptiness, even though I was making a six-figure income and living the highlife of going, doing, and buying whatever I wanted, whenever I wanted. I began to circle back to my original desire to become a psychotherapist.

I continued to try to conceive during this career transition.

While working as a sales manager, I had acquired tools from motivational speakers about goal-setting and creating vision boards; these, I found, blended well with my psychological training to increase coping skills, reduce stress, and create positive intention. After seven years of trying to conceive using alternative methods, I acquiesced to my husband's suggestion that we work with a physician who specializes in treating infertility. At the same time, I developed my clinical skills by attending training sessions that explored the healing use of rituals in psychotherapy. I incorporated everything that I had learned in my sales and psychology training and personal experiences to create a psychological treatment program to accompany my in vitro fertilization treatment protocol.

Before my infertility, I thought the process of conceiving a child was a spiritual endeavor that represented the love of two souls coming together to create a third. Now, this spiritual union had become a medical procedure that involved laying on a cold, hard, papered table with my legs up in uncomfortable metal stirrups while a man in a white lab coat stuck his rubber, gloved hands into my yoni bowl. He placed a vice that held the inner lips of my labia open wide, giving him an unobstructed view of the entrance of my vagina so he could do his job of assisting me in creating a baby. A sacred dream had turned into a medical nightmare.

Rituals I intuitively created for myself helped soothe my tattered soul that was bearing witness to a litany of poking, prodding, injections, and medications. I felt empowered as I selected the multi-sensory curatives to counteract the cold, painful realities of an infertility patient fraught with a myriad of diagnoses of what was ineffective or not working correctly. This pandora's box was filled with pathology seeking a man-made scientific cure. The rituals were a salve helping me center, relax, and visualize successfully becoming pregnant – and it worked! We were successful in conceiving our miracle baby after our first try at IVF, beating the thirty percent success rate.

Because of these experiences, I decided to specialize in working with people struggling with infertility. I became a support group leader for Resolve, a national infertility organization. I spoke at Resolve conferences, wrote articles for newspapers and magazines, and created a Reproductive Wellness Audio Series. The cornerstone of this work was sharing the Positive Intention Conception (PIC) Psychological treatment plan, which I developed while going through my infertility treatment. PIC has been embraced wholeheartedly; moreover, ninety percent of the women I have worked with over the last two decades were able to conceive when utilizing it, whereas they had been unsuccessful with medical intervention alone. The plan counteracts negativity, depression, and failure by using a multisensory approach that utilizes the neural pathways to access positive imaginal resources, both internal and external.

Three Steps of Positive Intention Conception (PIC) to transform from Maiden to a Mother

Step One: Identifying Your Fertility-Supporting Multisensory Pathways

There are two roads you can take. The longer road is to do guided imagery to your safe place that will assist you in making selections intuitively. There are several available online. With this method, after the guided imagery, you identify the dominant color(s) you saw and the sounds, scents, tastes, and textures you experienced through the imagery.

The shortcut is to ask yourself, "What are my fertility color(s) sounds, scents, tastes, and textures?" Intuitively pick the first selections that come to your mind. Do not overthink this. We are going to let the psyche guide us on the path to motherhood – not our ego, intellect, or logic. This psychological treatment plan supports and complements the medical treatment plan, in which ego, intellect, and logic *are* employed.

Sight-Fertility Color

Your fertility color supports you and helps you focus during this process. Every time you see this color you will know that the Universe is supporting you in your journey to motherhood.

Surround yourself with these colors. I purchased flowered sheets and a nightgown in my fertility colors of yellow and orange for my one-week bedrest after my treatment cycle. One client purchased a beautiful orange leather purse. Whenever she touched or looked at her purse, her thoughts were flooded with fertility, hope, and positive intention.

In the Resolve Infertility groups I led, each woman said her fertility color, and we sent her positive thoughts when we saw that color. This creates an empowering positive energy forcefield for the group participants.

Sharing one's fertility color with friends and family is very helpful. It gives them something concrete with which to communicate support, thereby replacing the anxiety and worry that results from seeing their loved one struggling. Many clients received fertility gifts from their friends and family in those colors – visual representations of their support and love.

Sound

Identify and download music or sounds that are comforting, soothing, and supportive to you. People have chosen children's lullabies, classical or new age music, Gregorian or goddess chants, ocean, stream, or birds chirping.

Fertility Scent

Our sense of smell is the most direct route to the brain, and we form immediate reactions based on memory and associations.

There is a wide range of fertility fragrances that people have chosen, including perfumes, baby lotion, or essential oils used in aroma therapy. If you are uncertain which scents to choose, health food stores have a large selection of essential oil samples so you can smell and decide which ones you are drawn to.

Taste

There are strong associations between smell and taste. For this sensory pathway, you want to identify foods that support your fertility. This could include favorite or comfort foods, and there may be overlap with the scents you have chosen. Examples people have chosen are berries, vanilla, lavender, orange, chocolate, and cinnamon rolls.

Touch

Identify the soothing textures you would like to accompany you on your fertility journey. Popular choices are soft blankets and clothing, warm sand, smooth rocks, flannel, velvet, corduroy, or silk fabric, to name a few.

Step Two: Create a Fertility Sanctuary

Once you have chosen your representations of sensory pathways to fertility, you then incorporate them into a special place, in or outside your living space, that you feel supports your fertility. This place needs a flat surface so you can create a fertility altar with your fertility-colored and textured fabric or material, candles, scented oils, or perfume. It will also include other special items.

Good Luck Charms or Fertility Symbols

Most of us who have experienced infertility have fertility good luck charms we or others have collected for us. Crystals, fertility goddesses, symbols or charms, pictures of ancestors, family members, babies, favorite landscapes or places, well-wishing cards, poetry, and positive affirmations or quotes are some options. I put my baby shoes on my altar and a small empty picture frame that was positively expectant. Some people also have put fresh flowers or jewelry on their altar. Whatever calls to you to support your transformation belongs there.

Candles

Use candles in your fertility color and/or fragrance; you are not limited to one fragrance. I had three fragrances: orange, vanilla, and musk. A popular color and scent choice is lavender. Sometimes it's a mix. One woman's color was white, and her fragrance was lavender. She had white and lavender candles. There are candles that represent various elements or purposes like healing, expecting a miracle, or wisdom. These are great additions to your altar. Candles are important to create a relaxing, spiritual atmosphere and thus are quite frequently used in religious ceremonies. Lighting a candle is the action to make something different happen. A burning fire is about transformation. When something is burning, it goes from one form to another.

Step Three: Create a Ritual

Now that you have gathered everything and created your fertility sanctuary and altar, you are ready to create a fertility ritual. Prepare yourself mentally for your fertility time or injections by anointing yourself with your scent, lighting your candles, and listening to your fertility sounds as you meditate on your intention of creating a child. After your injections, lie down, touch your chosen texture, and listen to a fertility-guided meditation found online or one you or your therapist have created specifically for you. Additions to this could be including your partner to participate by having them give you the injections or meditating as a couple on your intention to family build. One couple each chose what they needed at the time from a plate of stones with different supportive words and individually created a positive visualization. Create a ritual that feels supportive in expressing your spirituality and hopefulness.

It has been my clients' experience, as well as my own, that this step-by-step process of Positive Intention Conception is very helpful in counteracting the negative experience of infertility and its medical interventions. My clients report a greater sense of hopefulness, empowerment, and relaxation and decreased feelings of anxiety and depression. When following the suggestions and steps each person designs tailored to their needs and preferences, the focus shifts from diagnostic testing and diagnosing to identify the pathology to the multisensory elements of support and possibilities. Clients have reported for the first time that they were sad after their treatment cycle was over. They missed doing their fertility rituals, whereas previously, they were filled with anxiety, trepidation, resistance, and reluctance.

By creating more of a connection between the mind, body, and soul, you can empower and infuse the transformation from maiden to mother to unfold in a more embodied full flow of consciousness.

☾

Sara Rector LMFT is a Jungian Psychotherapist specializing in reproductive wellness who has been helping women become mothers for two decades. Sara shares with individuals, couples, and groups her psychological treatment plans that connect the soul with soma using rituals, positive intention, and dream-tending. Sara is also a sought-after speaker and writer of articles for Resolve, a national infertility organization; Fertility Summit; and Anji, a women's health and well-being website, sharing her expertise on such topics as Positive Intention Conception; Fractured Family Fairytales; Strategies to Help You Cope During the Holidays; Ceremonies and Rituals for Infertility and Pregnancy Loss; Keeping Your Marriage Alive; Relationship Issues and Infertility; How to Cope with Infertility as a Couple; Riding the Emotional Rollercoaster of Infertility; OVUM Donation (issues of disclosure); and Surviving Bed Rest.

She also has created a downloadable Reproductive Wellness Audio Series on her website:

circleoflifecounselingcenter.com/specialties/fertility

The Transcendent Power of Grief: Honoring the Alchemical Magic in Loss and Letting Go

LIZBETH RIZZO

She changed, but not overnight like in the books you read.
It happened over years, slowly and often painfully.
Sometimes brutally. But she did change.

~Author Unknown

Have you ever heard the expression "Deep grief changes a person"? It's true. Grief has absolutely changed me. My constitution is different now. I am energetically different than I was a year ago…4 years ago…12 years ago…34 years ago. Physically. Emotionally. Psychologically. Spiritually. Some changes rudely interrupted my life, in what I considered to be devastating ways. Other changes were subtle…gentle…nurturing…and well overdue. What is certain is that change and growth *are* inevitable. The nuances of **how** change happens is the fantastical mystery. Alchemy.

Merriam Webster describes alchemy as "a power or process that changes or transforms something in a mysterious or impressive way". Alchemical change IS mysterious, magical, transformative, destructive, creative. What I have experienced is that sacred transformational change occurs rarely without accompanying tower moments of Kali inspired destructive creative force. Deep complicated grief altered my patterns of sleeping, eating, daily routines, mental state, relational dynamics … and consequently caused a ripple effect of unexpected letting go of physical parts of me that no longer served. The energetic significance of this internal shift was astounding! True alchemical change requires monumental relinquishment of the previous state of being to create the magnificent energetic regeneration of a new state of being. A caterpillar transforming into a butterfly is a perfect example of this massive deconstruction of physical state to create a totally new being. That caterpillar knows that they have to surrender everything they know about their physical reality, to an unknown process that will absolutely and definitively decimate their current physical existence in order to continue living. This process is adequately described by the Latin expression *"solve et coagula"*… derived from *"solve,"* meaning to break down and separate, and *"coagula"* describing the process of bringing elements back together (coagulating) into a new, higher form.

Humans must do this too. Though for most, the experience may be less of an impressive physical shapeshifting and more of a subtle spiritual soulshifting. Yet, consider how humans shift from one lifetime to another. Relinquishing a physical body and life experience at death to enter into a whole new body and circumstantial experience in a reincarnated life rivals a butterfly transformation, yes? Life. Death. Rebirth. Shapeshifting. Soulshifting. Alchemical change. Thoughts about any of these topics can be influenced by our own personal beliefs about science and spirituality. Mind Body Soul. The holy trinity of existence. How do these seemingly separate and compartmentalized aspects of our selves shape who we are and our capacity to allow ourselves to change and morph in order to impressively transform? How do we "uncompartmentalize" our holy trinity and integrate our physical, mental, and spiritual selves to reflect the embodiment of growth, change and transmutation?

Thirty-four years ago I had a dream that I was walking along a dirt road in the dark. I saw strange lights in the sky and then unexpectedly found myself sitting at a round table inside a spacecraft. Two otherworldly beings have a pad of paper and a pen set out in front of me. They looked at me and nodded. "They" wanted me to write for them. When I woke up I wrote the dream down in my dream journal, as I do with all my significant and memorable dreams, but I didn't take it seriously. I felt the consequential importance of it. Yes. But I definitely did not prioritize this request, nor incorporate it into my daily life. As it was always in the back of my mind, I started scribbling notes here and there. I had stories to share. ***Where would I begin?***

Twenty-eight years ago I began dreaming of Snake energy...the energy of Transmutation and Rebirth. Lightning bolts of incredibly electric kundalini energy. Snake requested an awakening and attention to spiritual consciousness and a transmutation of my own existence. Beckoning me to dive deeper and explore all that is. ***What would it take?***

Twenty years ago I suddenly began dreaming frequently of whales and dolphins. Their energy also resonated vividly in my consciousness. I was being called again. I had a dream in which I was walking along a beach and a beautiful Orca with the sweetest soul walked out of the ocean in front of me, looked me in the eyes, handed me a pen, and nodded. As if to confirm that I understood the assignment this time. "They" wanted me to write for them. Surely the Universe was trying to get my soul's attention! Nudging me towards a lifelong dream to write, share stories, ancestral memories, spiritual musings and messages. It was time to share my truth and spill my magic. ***Where would I begin?***

It was so much easier to be the listener. THAT, I could do with ease. So much so that I made a career of listening, of caring, of helping others. I am a social worker, reiki master, death doula, and holistic wellness coach, combining many spiritual and therapeutic modalities of energetic healing, hypnotherapy, dream therapy, past life and ancestral healing, in my desire to help others thrive on their souls journey. I "hear", "dream", and "feel" messages from Spirit. I share messages with individuals as needed, but I have never shared messages through writing as I was "invited" to do. I realize I am engaged in a lifelong dance of allowing messages to flood in, and I am learning how to let my own self doubts wash away. Receiving and letting go. I asked myself over the years, what would it take? What kind of special magic would set me free of self doubts and allow myself to begin putting pen to paper? What would need to change in my personal psyche to allow Spirit to lead me, guide me, truly transform me? ***Where would I begin?***

I embarked on a deep dive into my own soul's journey, delved into my own shadow work and found out exactly what it would take for me to finally split open and accept the longstanding invitation for transmutation and transformation: Profound grief. The experience of gut-wrenching sorrow ... multiple, important losses over a short period of time, caused sequential tower moments so intricately and energetically entwined, that I began to write. I had to process everything in a meaningful way and allow myself the sacred space to engage body, mind, and spirit. The act of physically writing down my emotional response to concrete abject fact has been cathartic. Mysterious. Magical. It has changed me. The shocking and profound loss of loved ones and soulful relationships, initiated a shedding of skin, a peeling away and a letting go of all that did not serve my higher purpose. I had to let go. I had to forgive. I had to be willing to sit in my own darkest corners ... for it is in the dark that all our senses prickle with alertness and "crackle with light" in our process of awakening. Counselors and therapists believe that we can only take our clients and community as far as we have gone ourselves. Apparently, I had been wading on the shallow steps of life, so my Angels pushed me into the deep end of the pool. But hard! I have held the hands of the dying and witnessed their translucent passing into another realm. I have witnessed the miraculous remembrance of soul history, past lives and future possibilities. I have witnessed timelines mesh and merge. Therein lies the *magic*. We have to allow ourselves the time and space to experience all of it, in the moment. The highs and lows, joys, love and laughter and all the possible unplanned diversions that cause us to feel sadness, grief, and loss.

Tower Moments

Many experiences can cause a crumbling of your concepts and change life as you know it. Separation. Divorce. Traumatic incidence. Unexpected illness. Moving out of the home where you raised your children. Moving to new and unfamiliar places. Leaving behind treasured belongings. Untimely deaths of dearest loved ones, miscarriages, losing fur babies; relationship endings, loss/change of employment, retirement from lifelong careers. Whether or not changes are wanted, unwanted, necessary or not ... they can trigger a grieving process ... a dissonance between how you thought life was going to be and the reality of how it actually is. Any of these life-altering events would intrinsically change us in some way. We are forced to leave old patterns, notions and behaviors behind, requiring a shift in perspective and response, to accommodate a new reality. We are asked to grow into the change.

When I began having recurring clairvoyant dreams and noticed signs from Spirit that indicated I should move back to my hometown, I accepted the challenge to physically move cross country. I am blessed in so doing. Dreams are a treasured gift from Spirit! I was able to spend quality time with people I loved in a way I would not have had the chance if I stayed where I was. In order for me to experience this I had to change. I was humbled by the lessons and life experiences that met me. Humbled. Enlightened. Devastated. Decimated. Every fiber of my being vibrating to a chord I was not familiar with. Dissonance. That moment when I realized I wasn't in Kansas anymore. What I thought I knew about my Self shifted. Completely. The grief over multiple events concurrently occurring was overwhelming. In order to maintain my personal sense of self and navigate my emotional body, I made an agreement with myself to check in with Spirit daily. I asked myself "What will it take?" I prayed to my ancestors and Mother Mary every day, asking for whatever resources it would take for me to get thru the day. And the next day. And the day after that. Every day the remedied response was slightly different. Why? Expansion. My angels were tweaking my energy fields. Preparing me.

Grief, to me can be like the wind;
it can come like a soft breeze or hit like a tornado.
It affects everyone differently,
whether you are standing on top of a mountain
or in your valley,
it will always be felt!
Aaron Blanding, Teacher/Coach

How to transpose the energy of grief into a force for positive transformation...

- Spend time connecting to Spirit. Meditate. Breathe. Pray for your Highest Good. Surrender. Forgive.

- Honor your ancestors: cherish memories, photos, stories. Sit in places that honor your connections. Envision exchanging loving energy.

- Self Care: nourishment, sleep, healing salt baths, patience with yourself. Balance necessary alone time vs. time shared with others.

- Allow yourself to Feel. Give yourself time and space to release cathartic tears and emotions.

- Light candles, incense, essential oils, Sandalwood. Frankin-cense. Play music. These uplift / assist in creating sacred space for departing souls and for grieving hearts.

- Understand the underlying learnings and silver linings in the experience.

Can you hold gratitude and appreciation for the inevitable nature of change?

My father quite unexpectedly passed away in his sleep last Spring. Exactly the way he ordered it, though definitely not in his preferred timing. I stayed up all night almost every night that week, fraught with the thought of writing his eulogy. I could hear him pacing the hallway, playing his accordion, the scent of his cigarette in the air. He was just as shocked as we were. How do you encapsulate another human being's life experience in a way that honors their Spirit, their life journey … and the family experience? *I dreamt that I was handed a pen.* I sensed it was my father's hand. I woke up with a feeling of slight dread…whatever I write would not even come close to depicting all the feelings, all the experiences, the hardships, the joys, the arguments, or the soft quiet moments of understanding between us. I was too much in my own grief and sadness to think clearly. How do you put into words the unconditional love felt for your parents? It seemed the intricate dynamic between all of us was, in and of itself, an alchemical force of change.

Four days after we buried Dad, my mother quite unexpectedly had a stroke. I talked to her that morning before I left the house, reassuring her that it was the only day I needed to work that week. I received a call two hours later. Unbelievably, I experienced a tire blow out on my way to the hospital. I was upset, angry, and in mortifying disbelief about what was happening on the *only* day I had to be away from the family. It would take me a while to make peace with the fact that it seemed divinely orchestrated that I was not at home AND delayed getting to the hospital. There was purpose in the insanity, even though I could not see it in the moment. Mom did not want me interfering with her own transformation. Dying of a broken heart is a very real phenomenon that happens between soulmates. We understood that she did not want to be "here" any longer without her love. Our family painfully gathered again and with all that we could muster within us, offered her permission to go. We had to. There was no other way. With a flow of reiki and love in our hearts, we held her hands, shed our tears and played her favorite music as she took her last breath.

The Magic

In that exact moment Mom took her last breath, I vividly saw a pool of water in my parent's honeymoon location and I saw my young father lean in and extend his hand towards the water, and I watched my young mother rise up out of the water, reaching for her lover's hand. He was there to welcome her into their next spiritual adventure together. It was this precious parting gift that helped me transmute tremendous grief into loving expansion and acceptance of all that is.

Profound Love. Reverence for Life. Existential Appreciation. Willingness to Surrender...and an unwavering Faith in the unknown. The magical ingredients of Spiritual Alchemy.

This is where I begin.

☾

Lizbeth Rizzo, MA is a social worker, mother to four amazing humans, reiki master, holistic wellness practitioner, educator, death doula, author, dreamer, and social activist. She holds a Bachelor's in Social Work, Masters in Peace and Justice Studies. She holds multiple certifications in holistic healing modalities, conflict mediation, human rights education, domestic violence trauma/prevention.

Lizbeth intuitively combines modalities to effectively address the Mind, Body, Spirit with a holistic approach to personal and community wellness. Lizbeth holds special interest in the area of ancestral healing, fascinated by the implications and connective influence of past life experiences in our current reality. She is committed to addressing issues of social justice in our communities, with a special focus on individuals /families experiencing trauma related to domestic violence, human trafficking and homelessness.

Lizbeth currently lives in Toms River, NJ where she serves her community as a Domestic Violence Liaison with Providence House / Catholic Charities; and runs her private practice, Angelspace Therapies. To learn more about her work, visit:

angelspacetherapies.com

Alchemizing My Own Happiness

KARINA ROBBINS

For the first fifty years of my life, I remember thinking, *When is it going to be my turn to be happy?* I took care of everyone else and was so worried about them that I didn't have any time for me. I had six kids and an alcoholic husband and they kept me busy. I also worked full-time and went to school full-time. Looking back, I don't know how I had time for any of it. But it certainly kept me distracted from doing any work on myself or even thinking about what might make me happy.

When I was forty-two, my husband went to rehab (for the first time), and I was told that I needed to go to a thing called "Family Night." This was a group of spouses of alcoholics and addicts who would get together to talk about how best to support their loved ones. These people were all talking about a thing called codependency, which I had only vaguely heard of while working toward my bachelor's degree in psychology. Listening to the group, I thought, *Luckily, I don't have to deal with that, because I have enough on my plate already.* However, as these family members continued to talk about codependency, it became very obvious that I suffered from it as well. Hmm... What was I going to do about that? I already had enough to deal with. I ordered all the books anyway, but they hit just a bit too close to home and I stopped reading pretty early on.

See, the problem with learning things is that *then you know.* Once you know, you can't un-know, and you have to do something about it. At least, that is how my guidance works. So I stopped reading because I didn't want to know. If I knew, then I would have to make changes, and I wasn't ready for that, so my learning about codependency was shelved. This is called burying your head in the sand.

For the next several years I continued on, doing what I had always been doing. It wasn't really working for me, but it seemed to be working for everyone else in my life. One of the best things I did was start going to Al-Anon – a support group for friends and families of alcoholics and addicts. I learned so much there, had so many a-ha moments, things I thought I should have known. How had I missed all this foundational knowledge? I continued going for several years and it was just what I needed. My learning curve was slow and steady, just the way I needed it. I got a sponsor and continued to learn.

One day, I was complaining to my sponsor about my husband. She asked me, "What are the reasons you stay with him?" No accusations, no trying to sway me one way or the other. Just a simple question. Sadly, the only reason I could come up with was that I didn't want to hurt him by leaving. Her next question was, "How are you hurting yourself by staying?" This was one of those times when I knew. And now that I knew, what was I going to do about it? At the time, I was not ready to do anything. So, I stayed, trying to justify my decision and telling myself that I was fine.

Through a series of events that I can't even begin to explain, I ended up moving to Arizona by myself. I was offered a three-year contract there – an opportunity too great to decline – but my husband had no interest in living there. He helped me move, then returned to our Montana home. He told me he'd visit often (our kids were all grown and out on their own by this time), and perhaps do the snowbird thing, or stay two months in Montana, two months in Arizona, and so on.

I loved my new job and my new life. However, in my mind, I was still very much married. I was able to detach and let him decide to do whatever worked for him, but what worked for him was staying in Montana and drinking as much as possible. He had always blamed me for him not being able to drink, so this was his chance, and he took it. Though we were several states apart, I was still trying to manage his happiness.

I had moved to Arizona in August, and I loved it even more as the months passed. It was warm and sunny, even in the winter – something I had never experienced before, having grown up in Utah. Before I knew it, January was approaching, and with it, my fiftieth birthday. I couldn't believe it – fifty had sounded so old when I was eighteen! I was in serious denial about this milestone, which soon turned to melancholy about my life. If someone had told me when I was eighteen that my life would look like this at fifty, I would have cried. I was in a very unhappy marriage. I was out of alignment with my soul. I knew it and I couldn't un-know it. I truly started to see that things in my life had happened for me, not to me, and I needed to make some big changes, which was not going to be easy.

As I settled further into my life in Arizona (alone), and my husband continued to get worse (alcoholism is a progressive disease), I really started contemplating divorce. This was such a scary thought for me. I truly believed that I could not make it on my own financially. Looking back, this is quite funny as I had been the breadwinner for most (if not all) of the marriage and I was currently making a nice salary. It was just one of those lies that we tell ourselves, and then we come to actually believe it. One day in December, I had an epiphany: I had been living on my own in Arizona for four months, and I was doing just fine!

Hmm... It was another one of those things that once you know, you can't un-know. It took me a few more months and tons of courage, but I finally filed for divorce. It was one of the hardest things I have ever done and left me feeling alone and lonely. As this had been my second marriage, I also felt like I'd failed twice. For quite a while, I would view it as eighteen wasted years, but eventually, I came to understand it as a part of my life that made me who I am today.

Nine months after I moved to Arizona, I was officially single. I decided this was the time when I would finally get to be happy. The question was, what would make me happy? Sadly, I had spent so many years focused on everyone else that I didn't even know.

I was eager to learn, though.

I devoured books, took classes, listened to speakers, and went to workshops – all in an effort to figure out who I was, what I wanted, how to love myself, and how to be alone. None of this was easy. I finally faced my codependency and took a course on healing that. I was journaling, which helped me process my feelings and emotions. I started going to therapy, which helped by providing me an outlet to verbally process my thoughts and feelings, as well as someone to listen to me. Little by little, I was figuring out who I was and what I wanted out of life. I joined online communities and started traveling with the women in the communities. Very, very slowly, I transformed myself and my life. I made many mistakes along the way, but I was committed to listening to my intuition and changing course when I felt out of alignment.

Here's what I learned…

If I feel into things, use my intuition, and follow it, then my life goes smoothly, and I can relax and enjoy it. If I stuff my intuition down, like I did for my first fifty years, then my life will be difficult and a struggle. I really do have all the answers inside of me.

Today, nine years later, I am living the life of my dreams. I have my dream job, where I only work eight days a month. I have a beautiful home where I can spread out and feel comfortable and cozy. I have decorated it the way I want and love being at home so much. I have two cats that keep me company and make me laugh. I love sharing my life with these beautiful souls. I have curated beautiful friendships that are deep and fulfilling, and have many friends I travel with. I also have my own mastermind group that meets twice a month to share successes and challenges. We all can be authentically ourselves and be loved unconditionally. I travel solo sometimes, which is so empowering. I have beautiful relationships with all of my children, their spouses, and my grandchildren.

Ceremonies and rituals are an important part of my life. Moon ceremonies are among my favorite. Every new moon and full moon, I build a little altar and light a candle. I pull an oracle card and feel into that. Then I write down three things I would like to release (on a full moon) or manifest (on a new moon), as well as a few things that I am really grateful for and feel into those. It is so good for my spirit to take the time to do this twice a month.

I also look for the magic in my life. I am given so many signs, symbols, and synchronicities every day. I try to take the time to notice them. These are sent from my brother, my dad, my grandparents, my spirit team, my guides, and the ascended masters. There are so many signs, and I am so grateful when I recognize them. I know that they are guiding me, helping me know that I am not alone and that I am on the right path. I am so grateful for these breadcrumbs in my life.

I give gratitude every day for this life I have created (with help), and I celebrate where I am now, thank the Universe, and then let the Universe know that I am ready for more. Slowly, gently...

Nowadays, I consciously think, "This is my time to be happy and I am so grateful for my life and what it looks like now!" I look back on my life and see how things really did happen for me, not to me; I realize that while it may have taken me a while, once I started listening to my intuition it never steered me wrong. I am so grateful to be where I am today and able to experience true happiness. And, if you would have told my eighteen-year-old self that this is what my life would look like at fifty-nine, I would have cried with happiness, wondering if my life really could be this awesome!

Karina Robbins is a healer and an energy worker who is constantly searching for connection with others and more magic in her life. Karina works as a Certified Nurse Midwife and a Women's Health Nurse Practitioner. When she is not at the hospital, she practices Reiki, life coaching, and psychic mediumship; she is also becoming a yoga instructor. Her passions are traveling, self-development, scuba diving, reading, learning, and connecting with people. She runs a mastermind circle of several women who are interested in sharing their journeys in an authentic way. Karina is also the mother of six children and seven grandchildren and loves traveling and spending time with her family. She lives in Yuma, Arizona with her two cats and relishes this earthly existence each day. For more information, you may contact her at:

karinarobbins@aol.com

A Journey Through Layers of Alchemical Healing

HEIDI ROYTER

At the start of 2024, I committed myself to being one with my body and spiritually connected. So far, it has been a particularly challenging and transformative year, mirroring the alchemical process of turning base metals into gold. Alchemy, metaphorically, is the process of transforming our pain, struggles, and challenges into wisdom, growth, and enlightenment. Metals to gold, darkness to light.

Taking on a new and higher leadership role and struggling with my health have catalyzed my transformation. These life changes act as the furnace in alchemy, providing the heat and pressure necessary for deep change. I have been battling vertigo and dizziness for over five months, keeping this weakness close to home. These physical symptoms are like the impurities that surface, demanding attention and purification.

I feel like I am stuck behind a mask, one that says everything is fine while deep down feeling that things are out of my control and struggling with uncertainty. Despite this, I show up as best as I can at home and work, taking care of my responsibilities because that is what I must do. At my core, I feel stuck in a deep abyss, circling as if a black hole resides in the depths of the unknown. This abyss represents the "Negredo" stage, where everything is reduced to chaos and dissolution, where old structures break down to make way for new growth.

Throughout my journey, I have faced the struggles of embracing self-love, acceptance, and the transformative power of alchemy. My experiences with vertigo and dizziness force me to confront my deepest fears and emotions, challenging over two decades dedicated to my personal growth and spiritual connection.

In my professional life, I work as a leader, inspiring others to embark on their own alchemical journeys and guiding them through. The previously mentioned struggles provide me with a deep well of empathy, allowing me to connect with them. I study various healing modalities, including mindfulness, meditation, and energy healing, which I integrate into my life and work. My commitment to self-growth is unwavering. I have attended numerous workshops, retreats, and training programs to deepen my understanding of healing. These enrich my perspective and provide me with the tools to navigate my journey. My story is not just about overcoming challenges, but embracing them as fuel for change. I have learned that true healing is an ongoing process, requiring continuous self-reflection, adaptation, and courage.

My aim is to show others that even in the darkest times there is potential for growth. My journey is a testament to the power of resilience, self-love, and turning life's dark moments into light.

In the depths of my current struggles, I feel like an outsider in both my body and surroundings. Trying to control my mental, emotional, and physical state, yet finding no control at all. I understand that I give so much unconditional love, compassion, and understanding to others but not enough to myself. I see that I have created these experiences out of a longing for unconditional love and acceptance. I need to consistently direct this energy toward giving myself what I feel like I've been lacking.

Deeper within this dark abyss, I'm realizing that connecting behaviors embedded in me for so long and turning my feelings toward myself is creating friction. This friction creates the heat necessary for transformation. Conflicting with myself means losing people in the process and facing the truth about change. Sadness and loneliness are deep, and I'm sitting with myself trying to declutter thoughts, feelings, and emotions within me.

My turning point is emerging during this particularly challenging time. I'm forced to slow down and confront my physical and emotional state. It is intense self-reflection, much like the process of calcination, where impurities are burned away. My physical symptoms are a manifestation of deeper emotional and spiritual issues that need to be addressed.

As I ascend into my true self, I am – much like cleaning my house – removing all the clutter, understanding each piece and how it served me in the past, and why it no longer serves me today. Dusting off shelves, searching deep within the corners of the cabinets for anything obscured, and disposing of what I have been hiding from myself. Observing these pieces – a lack of worthiness, a fear of being seen. Further into the cleaning process, I begin to reorganize and restructure the shelves that make up myself. What truths are worth keeping, and what false beliefs do I need to get rid of? As every shelf becomes cleaner, I know I become closer to being whole. As I mop the floor, it begins to reveal a clear path forward.

This process is not easy. It requires facing painful truths about myself and my past. A period of "Dissolution," where old structures and beliefs are being broken down. Confronting my fears and insecurities head-on. Through this process, I'm beginning to see the light at the end of the tunnel. This light represents "Conjunction" to me, where various aspects of the self are integrated and unified.

One of the most significant moments in my journey is acknowledging my fear of being seen. This fear has kept me from fully expressing myself and embracing my true potential. By facing it, I can release it and step into my true self. This "Fermentation" stage is where new life and potential begin to emerge.

Continuing to work on myself, I notice changes in my external world. Relationships that are no longer aligned with my true self are falling away, making space for new, more authentic connections. My physical symptoms are beginning to improve as I address the underlying emotional and spiritual issues. I'm starting to feel a sense of peace and clarity that I have never experienced before. This very much reflects the "Distillation" stage in alchemy, where purity and clarity are achieved.

Transformation is a testament to the power of resilience. It is a challenging yet profoundly rewarding journey that I'm committed to seeing through to discover the light within myself. I'm currently navigating through another layer of my alchemical healing journey, and I want to share the actionable steps I am taking so you may apply them in your own life.

Here are the steps you can take if you are on your own alchemical transformation journey:

1. Acknowledgement and Awareness

Step 1: Self-Reflection

- What I Am Doing: I take time each day to reflect on my thoughts and feelings. Journaling is a powerful tool for this process. I write down my emotions, fears, and hopes, bringing unconscious thoughts to the surface.

- What You Can Do: Set aside time each day to journal your thoughts and feelings. Reflect on your emotions and experiences to gain a deeper awareness of your inner state.

Step 2: Honest Inventory

- What I Am Doing: I conduct an honest inventory of my life. I identify areas where I feel stuck or unfulfilled and ask myself why these areas are not aligning with my true self. This is the initial phase of acknowledging what needs to change.

- What You Can Do: Take an honest look at your life. Identify areas where you feel discontented or misaligned with your true self. Write down these observations and explore why these areas need transformation.

Tools to Consider: Journal, quiet space, willingness to be honest with yourself.

2. Declutter and Purify

Step 3: Letting Go

- What I Am Doing: I start letting go of what no longer serves me. This includes toxic relationships, old beliefs, and habits that keep me from growing. I visualize these as impurities in the alchemical process that need to be burned away.

- What You Can Do: Begin the process of letting go of anything that no longer serves your highest good. This could be toxic relationships, limiting beliefs, or unhelpful habits. Visualize releasing these impurities from your life.

Step 4: Mindful Meditation

- What I Am Doing: I practice mindfulness and meditation to help clear my mind. I focus on my breath and allow thoughts to come and go without attachment, purifying my mind and emotions.
- What You Can Do: Incorporate mindfulness and meditation into your daily routine. Focus on your breath and practice letting go of thoughts without attachment. This will help purify your mind and emotions.

Tools to Consider: Meditation app, quiet space, visualization techniques.

3. Dust Off and Restructure

Step 5: Identify Core Values

- What I Am Doing: I identify my core values and what truly matters to me. I dust off these values and bring them to the forefront of my life, recognizing my true worth and what I stand for.

- What You Can Do: Identify your core values and prioritize what truly matters to you. Reflect on these values regularly and align your actions with them.

Step 6: Set Intentions

- What I Am Doing: I set clear intentions for how I want to live my life. These intentions align with my core values and true self. I write them down and revisit them regularly.

- What You Can Do: Set clear, intentional goals for your life that align with your core values. Write them down and review them regularly to stay focused and aligned.

Tools to Consider: Core values worksheet, intention-setting journal.

4. Deep Cleaning

Step 7: Confront Hidden Fears

- What I Am Doing: I confront and address hidden fears and insecurities. This is the hardest part of the process, akin to deep cleaning. I seek professional help if necessary, such as therapy or counseling, to guide me through this.

- What You Can Do: Face your hidden fears and insecurities head-on. Seek professional support if needed, such as a therapist or counselor, to help you navigate this challenging part of the process.

Step 8: Emotional Release

- What I Am Doing: I allow myself to feel and release pent-up emotions. Crying, screaming, or writing about my pain helps in the emotional release, which is crucial for deep healing and transformation.

- What You Can Do: Allow yourself to fully experience and release your emotions. Find healthy ways to express and release your feelings, such as journaling, crying, or physical activity.

Tools to Consider: Therapist, counselor and/or coach, emotional release exercises, support group.

5. Integration and Alignment

Step 9: Align Actions with Values

- What I Am Doing: I ensure that my daily actions align with my core values and intentions. This creates coherence between my internal beliefs and external actions, leading to a more authentic and fulfilling life.

- What You Can Do: Align your daily actions with your core values and intentions. Make conscious choices that reflect your true self and desired path.

Step 10: Create Rituals

- What I Am Doing: I develop daily or weekly rituals that reinforce my values and intentions. This could be a morning meditation, gratitude practice, or regular exercise. Rituals help in integrating new habits into my life.

- What You Can Do: Create daily or weekly rituals that support your values and intentions. These practices will help you stay grounded and aligned with your goals.

Tools to Consider: A planner or calendar; reminders for rituals; support from friends or family.

6. Embrace the Journey

Step 11: Accept Imperfection

- What I Am Doing: I embrace my imperfections and understand that stumbling is part of the journey. Alchemy is not about achieving perfection, but about continuous transformation and growth.

- What You Can Do: Accept your imperfections and view them as part of your journey. Understand that growth involves making mistakes and learning from them.

Step 12: Trust the Process

- What I Am Doing: I trust in the process of life and my own resilience. I release the need for control and allow life to unfold naturally. This trust reduces anxiety and helps me stay present.

- What You Can Do: Trust in the process of life and your inner resilience. Let go of the need for control and allow life to unfold as it should. This will help you remain calm and present.

Tools to Consider: Affirmations, mindfulness practices, support network.

Helpful Tips to Remember:

- I am patient with myself. Transformation takes time.

- I celebrate small victories along the way and acknowledge my progress.

- I seek support when needed. I do not have to do this alone.

- I stay committed to the process, even when it gets tough.

By acknowledging, purifying, and restructuring my inner self, I can transmute my pain into wisdom and align with my true purpose. This will be the light at the end of the darkness. Remember, there is no destination; there is only now. I embrace the process, trust my journey, and allow myself to shine like gold.

Within this alchemical journey, I know that every step I take is a step toward becoming one with myself. The path is challenging, but rewarding. By trusting the process, I discover a deeper connection with myself and the world around me. This journey is about finding the light within and letting it shine brightly. I have the power to transform my life and create a reality that aligns with my true essence. The transformative process has changed my life in ways I never imagined.

☾

Heidi Royter is the energetic President and COO in corporate America's long-term care industry, with a flair for overseeing business operations and fostering employee growth. She also works privately with individuals, empowering them to achieve their personal and professional dreams.

Heidi's journey took her through UNLV, where she studied Business Management. She holds an associate's degree in Mind-Body Transformation and is also a certified yoga instructor and clinical hypnotherapist. Her vibrant energy and direct approach have helped countless employees and clients experience significant personal and professional growth and transformation.

Passionate about recognizing and overcoming self-defeating behaviors, Heidi supports her clients in setting positive intentions and embracing new patterns of thinking and doing. She finds joy in guiding others to celebrate their successes, live well, and be free. Whether she's working in corporate America or in private sessions, Heidi's uplifting spirit and dedication make her a beacon of inspiration and positive change. In her spare time she likes to read, write, make jewelry, and spend time with her family.

heidi.royter@outlook.com

Echoes of Shadow

AURORA LUNA STAR

We have all heard Covid stories of people stranded thousands of miles from home, and of those in the hospital alone, sequestered from their loved ones. In my parents' case, both scenarios were true. While my parents were stuck in Los Angeles because of the pandemic, Dad had a bad experience (at a famous hospital) and, as no visitors were permitted, thought he was going to leave the planet alone. When we heard how scared he was, my three sisters and I immediately began trying to figure out how to get our parents back to New York. I told them I would "pick up" Mom and Dad and help them get home. It made sense since I was in Arizona and had only a dog for a child, whereas they were all married and each had three children.

The flight from Phoenix to LA is only an hour and twenty minutes, but it was incredibly stressful. I flew first class with the intention of having distance between myself and other passengers. Instead, I was not only stuck with someone next to me, they were constantly blowing their nose. As I was on my way to my eighty-year-old mother and my nearly eighty-three-year-old father, who was navigating leukemia, I was beyond upset. I spoke to a flight attendant, who offered me no solace whatsoever. I went back to my seat and began to cry. And then I began to bawl. And then I stopped and took a deep breath – or as deep as one could with a mask on – and knew everything was unfolding in Divine order. I just needed to have faith. There was nothing I could do except (accept) surrender.

I got to my parents okay; I also, upon arrival, threw all my clothes in the laundry. I wanted to make sure that Dad wasn't going to get any more ill than he already was. I was definitely in fear of bringing the virus to either or both of them, but thankfully, all was well. The goal now was to get them ready to fly out the next day to New York and get Dad into a well-known cancer hospital in Manhattan.

Dad was not doing so well. He had trouble walking on his own, and he was just so frail-looking. It was challenging to see him, the rock of our family, this way. It was like witnessing the decomposition of a mighty oak. Yet we made it through airplanes and airports and arrived in New York safe, sound, and COVID-free. And that's when the real fun began.

My oldest sister took Dad to the hospital to meet his new doctor and determine what treatments they would try. A man of routine, my father had been seeing the same doctor in Los Angeles for more than twenty years, and he had no interest in starting over at this stage of the game. In fact, after that last hospital visit out there, Dad had decided he was done with hospitals, he was done with treatment, he was done with all of it.

Now, this new doctor was saying that if he refused treatment he would have seven days to live. I was with Mom when she got that information. Her face turned white. I could see the shock settling into her central nervous system. Seven days. That was no time at all.

My mother and sisters were pleading with him to change his mind. I, on the other hand, stood as the sentinel, guarding him in every moment. If he was ready to go, and this is how he wanted to go, I was going to make damn certain that no one would get in his way.

I was the witness on his DNR. It felt so odd. Here I was, the baby in the family, protecting his wishes and signing the documents. I was holding the field on his behalf. I had compassion for Mom and my sisters but I wasn't going to let them argue with him, at least not without me there to protect him. I felt it was my responsibility, as my beliefs have always been grounded in knowing that the soul is eternal and the body is just a vehicle we borrow for a period of time.

On night four of seven, I was behind a closed door in my parent's guest bedroom, attending a membership meeting online. Mom was on the phone in their bedroom, and my eldest sister and Dad were in the living room.

I was just about to start a meditation when I heard her yelling at him. I was boiling inside. I was boiling because she waited to get him alone to beg him to go to the hospital and resume treatment. I couldn't even address what was happening in that moment, other than to open the door and tell her that all my clients could hear her yelling through the door.

When the membership group was complete, I opened the door to find my sister making arrangements for my dad to get a blood transfusion and see the doctors.

That night is forever burned in my memory because Dad changed his soul contract in that moment, and he did it for her. And while that was, of course, his prerogative and his life to choose, to this day, I am not really sure that he was doing it because he wanted to. And I resented her for it.

I was initially going to stay in New York for two weeks, and then the unthinkable happened. Mom asked me to stay an additional two weeks. I wanted to say no. It was very hard to be there. Dad was up all night and slept all day and he needed a lot of help with pills and meals. He was an absolute bear to Mom and just angry in general. He was angry that he was dying, yes, but I could feel that more than angry, he was afraid.

Nearly in tears, I called my dogsitter and asked to FaceTime with Finn. I couldn't stand to be away from my best fury friend and emotional support for another two weeks; I also knew that staying meant being in the dense energy of fear, anger, and death. I could meditate from that day until the following year, but nothing was going to align my energy. I was swimming in low vibrational frequencies and surviving on pizza and ice cream. I was in an emotional pit with all of them, but I couldn't bring myself to say no. Mom never asked for anything. *Anything.* She always would say that things were fine. Well, we were definitely a quarter-past fine and half-past insanity. Things were feeling dire.

Dad managed to hold on for six whole months. Again, I just don't know how he did it. I can't fathom the never-ending appointments, needles, trips from one side of Long Island to the other, or into Manhattan. It was never-ending discomfort, and he chose it for as long as his body could take it.

He went into the hospital right before Christmas Eve. Things weren't looking so good. The doctors could see he had pneumonia, which is usually a sign that the body is letting go. We had a family Zoom meeting with the doctors on Christmas about starting hospice. I had just finished running a six-day retreat and I was so filled with light that all of my shadow was rising to the surface; I didn't even know it, though, until the trigger came.

My oldest sister told me and my other sisters that when she was with Dad he kept asking for help. This upset her so much that she wanted to talk to the doctors about getting him more blood transfusions. That's when my shadow reared its ugly head, with no mercy and absolute rage. In my mind, it was already her fault that he had endured the last six months of pain and suffering. And now she wanted to start blood transfusions after the doctors had clearly stated there was nothing more that could be done?! I uttered words to her that you shouldn't even say to your worst enemy ... and I couldn't fathom at that moment how much I would pay for saying those words.

I told her that if she spoke to the doctors she would be dead to me, that she needed to grow up and let him go. I was out of my heart and out of my mind with grief for him, and I took it out on her. The worst part was that, in that moment, I meant it. I meant it so much. I was so angry with her. It took me six months to even find compassion for where she was, to see his passing and the pain of loss through her lens.

Within four months of Dad's funeral, her husband was diagnosed with liver and pancreatic cancer. I was so filled with shame that by the time I got over myself, my triggers, and my perception of what happened between her and our father, I had no way of providing any support. Not to my brother-in-law, not to my niece or nephews, and most of all, not to my sister. The damage of my words had been done, and there was no good time to even attempt an apology. I didn't want to make anything about me. I didn't want her to have to process the emotions of what I had said to her. I wanted her to be able to focus on her family.

And last month, he died.

My mom is the one who called me to let me know. But I knew already. My brother-in-law had reached out to me energetically three days before he left his body. I could feel his presence around me. I set an intention to project a higher aspect of myself to stay with him in the hospital and be with him while he was in an in-between state of energy. I lit candles and prayed for him for two days. And on the third day, early in the morning, as I was waking up, I could hear the frequency of an Archangel letting me know that he had crossed over.

I loved him. He wasn't just a "some guy my sister married." There was a lot of history there. Some of it was hard, but most of it was good. He traversed a lot of grief and challenges in this life. I am still lighting candles and praying for the elevation of his soul, as I also send loving prayers for my sister and her children, whom I love so very much.

I recently realized that if I had not blown up at my sister over Dad, I probably would have over her husband. Many things unfolded that were essentially none of my business; I feel that had I been present, I most likely would have made things much worse by not being able to keep my opinions to myself.

My family has always been my biggest classroom. I realize how far out of alignment I am when I see my old triggers come up. It's hard to think that you have come so far on a spiritual journey, only to become ten years old again the second I am in that family field of consciousness.

My mom and I talked a lot about what unfolded with my oldest sister. Mom wanted to understand why it was so hard for me to hold back harmful words. In truth, I'd known my whole life that my temper was my Achilles Heel, and that if I was going to live a happy and fulfilled life, something would have to shift.

My response to her was simple. I experienced trauma before I could even speak. I had to scream to protect myself. I had to scream to survive. And even though that wasn't true anymore, the body remembers. It's an automatic firing system. Dad had needed protecting in the mind of my inner child, and so she, my inner child, erupted.

My sisters are my parents' biological children. None of them experienced trauma. They all had suburban, middle-class lives. I had that too, don't get me wrong. But I also went back and forth between my birth mother and my family for the first eight years of my life, and the abuse that took place shaped the life I am still healing today.

☾

Aurora Luna Star is an Inter-dimensional Channel specializing in Starseed Akashic Readings, Sound Healing Activations, and Personal Empowerment. Through her channel, Aurora connects with The Elders of the Cosmos, accessing light codes via sound, messages, images, and light language. Her purpose is to guide you toward embracing your fullest potential, acting as a catalyst for your personal growth and transformation. Aurora's greatest joy is empowering each person to realize their unlimited nature and see themselves as the master beings that they already are.

auroralunastar.com

Re-membering Our Sacredness

MARILYN MILLER USSELMAN

We are all born with a wild woman inside who is free of fixed false beliefs and social conformity. We were fearless as we entered this world. We came because we agreed to be the change-makers. We are here to break ancestral/generational patterns that do not serve our authentic selves. My wild woman is fiercely wild and filled with magic. She glows with a love of adventure and a touch of defiance. She goes by the moniker Isador.

I hung onto Isador as long as I could, but, like everyone, I was pushed through the cattle shoots of the socially acceptable behaviors and belief systems of our Society. We all lose touch with our alchemy and become more clonelike. We are taught that it is not safe to be a dreamer. We are pressured into doing and are taught to stop being. Can you recall, as you were getting ready to graduate high school, how many times you were asked what you were going to do with your life? We are forced to learn the same way, and our success is measured against each other by level of education, income, and material possessions. If we struggle to find our place in the automated system, we are labeled difficult, slow, or lazy. It appears as if

Society rewards those who are quick to turn off the light of individuality and assume the role of people-pleasing mannikins. Authenticity and truth are sacrificed for herd mentality.

Our Alchemy is reduced to shadows. We become careful about sharing our innermost thoughts and dreams for fear of being labeled. We question our intuition and make ourselves small. We begin to believe that there must be something wrong with us for desiring and longing for something different.

This longing became increasingly difficult to ignore. My wild woman clamored for love and attention. She desired to be set free from her entombment in the shadows. I felt like this void wanted to be filled but I wasn't sure how to do that. As I was leaving the mother stage and entering my crone stage, I started to search out energy-based practices. I have collected magic rocks and crystals since I was knee-high to a grasshopper. The family joke is that my bedroom could withstand any tornado due to the rock collection I have in there. The house will be gone but the bedroom will still be there.

I have always been attuned to the elements of nature. Water calms me, fire transmutes all things that no longer serve me, air cleanses me, and earth grounds me. I started searching for classes that were off the beaten path. I became certified in Reiki and love to do long-distance healing for others. I then took a dowsing course so I could clear spaces. It was then that I became fully aware of my animal guides. When I noticed that a beautiful white wolf showed up whenever I was dousing, I took an animal communication course. Before I knew it, I was on a merry-go-round, taking course after course and gaining more knowledge so I could set up my spiritual business. This was about confidence; I felt I couldn't charge for my services because I wasn't an expert yet. I didn't know how to explain what I did, therefore I didn't feel like I had anything of monetary value to offer.

One of my biggest a-ha moments came during a course to become a mind, body, spirit practitioner. We were told to walk the labyrinth sometime that week, and since I didn't want to walk it with anyone present I found myself on the last day standing outside while others went in. One woman, who was struggling to find her way out, decided there was a mistake in the labyrinth. Before I knew it, I was walking straight across it to the center and guiding her out. When the class reconvened, we were asked if we all walked it, and we all answered yes. I counted my rescue attempt as my walk.

The instructor then looked around and said, "How you walked the labyrinth is how you show up in life."

I was stunned. I realized right then and there that I'd always been a rescuer and problem-solver. By constantly offering the solutions I saw as obvious, I was not allowing others their struggle; I was interfering with valuable life lessons, thus helping to ensure they would continue to repeat them. They had to learn to be present and do their own work in order to transform.

Another a-ha moment came when I went to a healing retreat in Sedona a couple of months later. One of the exercises was about the stories we tell. Everyone, except me and a few others, shared their stories. The lady running the retreat came over to me and asked what my story was. I told her I didn't have one, but she kept asking until I became irritated.

"I don't tell anybody anything" I exclaimed, "I don't have a story!"

She leaned in real close, looked me straight in the eyes, and said, "That *is* your story!"

Bam! Light bulb turned on. I was an expert at being invisible, at hiding in plain sight.

I paused for a while to put these learnings to use in my life. I was still feeling like I was missing a connection to nature and discovered the earth-based practices of shamanism. This is where I felt at home. I identified with the elements and tutelary animals of each direction. Just like humans, our stone relatives, plant relatives, and animal relatives are all connected in the circle of life. I believe we survive together or not at all.

Though I felt very connected, my little inner critic kept chattering. "You aren't doing it right," it said, "you aren't pronouncing or toning the words correctly, people are going to judge, this won't work." I became self-conscious whenever I tried to go into ceremony and stopped opening my Mesa. I kept taking courses but wasn't putting it into action. I didn't know how to interrupt the signal from the inner critic.

Eventually, I traced all this back to an extremely traumatic event (or "impact moment," as Melissa Kim Corter calls them) I had suffered around the age of sixteen. That was when my wild woman became silent and encased in the shadow and the inner critic took over. The whole landscape of my life was altered. I didn't feel safe anymore. I had other impact moments during my mother stage as well. These moments and the emotions tied to them were pushed further down into the shadows.

These impact moments can rip us apart. We feel broken and fragmented. I think shadow work is like building a quilting collage or tapestry. We start out whole and then parts of us are torn out. In quilting, we take large pieces of fabric and cut them up into smaller pieces. We take those "broken" pieces and stitch them back to-gether. We treat those smaller pieces with patience and love and sometimes we swear a little as we create the collage. They are stitched into a beautiful pattern which is uniquely different from the original fabric. It is created from the whole cloth, but it changes when it comes back together. I think this is how shadow work shows us that those pieces of our whole still have value. They don't fit back where they originally did, but we use them to create a new tapestry. The pattern is different because we are different. We are like the water in a river. You never touch the same water twice. We learn from these events/moments and use them to forge something stronger. We meld the lessons into healing stories that we need to share be-cause we agreed to live an authentic life. We are no longer afraid of the naked truth. We heal ourselves by sharing our truth and holding space for others to step into the shadows to retrieve the torn and tattered pieces of ourselves that we thought were lost forever.

This is the true sacredness of the Alchemy of the Wild Woman. She shows others that we don't have to fear the rebirth of our ourselves, that it is safe and sacred to lean into the emotions and feelings we have pushed down into the shadows. Once we realize we are safe to experience life through the wisdom of the crone, the com-passion of the mother, and the openness of the maiden, our shadow work will no longer be something we dread. We will choose to enter this space because we know the growth will be exponentially multiplied on the other side.

I did not know how to deal with my fear of the shadow and how to retrieve those pieces of my soul. I have found someone who can mentor me through that fear by teaching me to be present and to lean into it. Melissa Kim Corter is that person. I feel vibrationally connected to her style of teaching about the shadow and the ego. She taught me how to get quiet and centered with her hypno-nidras. Over time, I was able to get into the brain state quicker and easier. I had tried EFT technique many times in the past and could never get the connection. It felt like I had a short in my electrical system because it didn't do anything. Then I tried the intuitive tapping that Melissa created and I couldn't believe how things started to shift when I went through the process.

I am drawn to people who are not all love and light. I like mentors who are real. Life can get messy, and I tend to shut down my connection with Spirit and nature when I am stressed. I stop using my tools and let my monkey brain take over. I am a fire sign and I tend to blaze through my stress. I am a shallow breather by nature.

I am learning to reset my nervous system by recognizing when I am starting to go over the cliff of doing instead of being. There are three things I try to do on a consistent basis: breathwork, creative endeavors, and practicing gratitude.

I have incorporated different breathwork techniques – some simple, some complex – into my daily routine. One of them, which I use to get back into connection, is to just become aware of my breath as I inhale and exhale. I don't change the rhythm or rate; I just remain aware. After a few breaths I tune into the space where the inhalation switches to an exhalation. I don't try to expand this space; again, I am just aware of it. I do the same at the bottom of my breath, the space where exhalation changes to inhalation. I try to do this for a few minutes, outside in nature, if possible. It is amazing how chill I am afterward.

I have also figured out that I need to do something creative to keep myself in my natural rhythm. I have many projects in process and a long waiting list of those to be started. When I create something for someone, I use my intuition to guide the process. I have started to charge the item with Reiki, then infuse it with love and the essence of my wild woman. She is my inner shaman. She is a medicine woman.

Every day I call in Spirit, and my support team made up of Archangels, Angels, Fairies, animal guides, and spirit guides. I thank them for their loving support. I ask for their help in being an open and hollow bone, open to receiving any messages, ask that no animals lose their life to deliver these messages, open to receiving abundance and to be at zero—free of judgment, attachment, and expectations. I then ask for their help with surrounding those on my prayer list with their warm embrace.

We are the ancient wisdom-keepers. We came to be the change-makers. We have a vibration or beat that connects us to each other and to Mother Earth. There is a sacredness in that connection. We can only make change in the world if we do the inner work for ourselves. Plant your seeds. Claim your sacredness, honor your path, and share your stories, my beautiful wild women. Re-member who you are, the Alchemist of change and healing

☾

Marilyn Miller Usselman grew up in Montana and has never left. She does loves to travel, though, especially to take pictures of landscapes and wildlife, and is on a quest to visit sixty-three national parks. As a registered nurse of thirty-two years, she has been involved with helping others heal and transition, which has led her to pursue her self-healing journey and create life-work balance. Marilyn is fascinated with energy work, and has several guilty pleasures, including dark chocolate, NHRA drag races and NASCAR races, and family get-togethers to share traditions. She loves spending time with her boxer, Stryder, her grandpup, Scoot, and her son, Chase. Marilyn's chapter in *The Wild Woman's Book of Alchemy* is her first published work.

The Decision to Leave

KIMBERLY WEYAND

Someone recently asked me how difficult it was to make the decision to leave my husband. I'm not exactly sure because it feels like the decision was made for me. If I wanted to live and keep my kids safe, I had to go. I'm not really sure when I *consciously* made that choice, but at some point, I had to ask myself, "Is it worth the risk to stay?"

In the weeks leading up to my leaving, Hugh's physical, mental, and verbal abuse had escalated. But when it was directed at the girls, that was it. I locked us all in the bathroom and called one of my dearest friends, who happened to be a juvenile judge. His words struck me like a club. "You have a duty and a responsibility," he said, "to keep those children safe. I trust you will make the right decisions." The questions that followed were many, and though some remained unanswered, I had come to trust this friend more than my husband. It's still quite overwhelming when I think about it.

After hanging up with my friend I called the police and described the situation. "Are there any guns in the home?" they asked, shocking me to the very core. I had not truly considered that he would use them on us.

"Yes," I responded with a sickening feeling in my stomach. They were stored in the side of the house where he was at the moment. He had been sleeping in the guest room in that wing of the house, and the guns were in the closet of the room next to him. I honestly couldn't answer any other questions, like how many, or if they might be loaded at the time. I knew he used to be careful about that sort of thing, but now I wasn't sure.

We stayed in the locked bathroom while awaiting the police to arrive. Hugh was calm when he answered the door, but I could tell from his tone that he was irritated that they wanted him to leave the home. He stood firm that he would not. With guns in the home, it was now up to me to "keep those children safe!"

Fortunately, I had already been preparing for this night for some time, including talking to someone at Women Helping Women and reading books on planning the separation. Suggestions included packing one season of clothes in black garbage bags and stowing them where they wouldn't be found by the abuser, as well as stashing cash away on a weekly basis, in a way that would not arouse suspicion. This had proved tricky, however, because he found some of my storage spots without letting me know. They also recommended letting a few "safe" people know about the issues, then erasing any correspondence. This felt eerily like leaving a suicide note, considering the danger if he found any trace of them on the computer that we shared. In fact, after I confronted him about porn in the emails, he had become diligent about clearing the cache and could possibly find what I deleted if I wasn't careful.

Now, after being given a few options by the police, I quickly moved into action. I quickly grabbed a few things for me and the girls, jammed the clothes in bags, and hurried them into our van. The police watched Hugh in the kitchen, and I noticed one officer leaning against the counter in front of the knife block.

I pulled out my phone and called the local camper repair shop. The last detail of my plan was housing. Where would we live if we didn't have income or resources? After careful consideration, I'd decided to take the popup camper and had it fully serviced and made sure it was travel-ready, should the time arrive. Now was the time, but it was still within the locked fence of the repair shop. It would be ready in the morning, they assured me, but were closing for the day. What do I do until then? I knew the way to a local women's shelter, as I had been there for advice, but it was full to capacity, as was every hotel in town. I kept making calls, trying to find a solution, but I was stumped.

Then it hit me: these girls love camping so much, so maybe I could make the van a "camper" for the night. But where to go? I didn't want to be too far from the camper, so we could get it as soon as the shop opened and head south to family and treasured friends. It had been hard, being honest with loved ones about what a nightmare our marriage had become. By that point, I had already tried counseling, but it was clear that wasn't going to help.

So many people rallied around us. My big brother invited us to stay "on the farm" at his place and he would help protect us if it came to that. Several family members were teachers in the schools the kids would attend, so they assured me they would remain safe. My sister said her prayers with me and wished me luck, but was a little off the path I had planned to take. I let her know our stops and travel timeline. It eased our minds to know that God was watching over us.

We stopped to pick up a few essentials for the night and a few extra pillows at the Walmart across from the camper shop. One of my girls asked a serious question while waiting in line.

"What if Daddy finds us?"

I quickly hushed her and gave her a hug, then awkwardly shrugged it off to the clerk and bagged our stuff. A couple overheard us, though, and I was on high alert when they motioned me over to where they stood with a small group. Their friends wandered off as the couple suggested I park my van between some of their RV campers.

"Aha!" I said, realizing that these were the Shriners in town this week, taking up all the hotel rooms!

"Yes," he confirmed as he kindly offered to have coffee with us in the morning, as well as let the kiddos use their potty if needed during the night.

The kids and I cried as we thought and planned out our next steps. I had been protecting them from seeing or hearing the offensive language their father was using on me and the hurtful things he had done in the past. This wasn't the time to bring all that up, but in my mind, it solidified my resolve that this would be it. Leaving him for the last time.

In the weeks leading up to this, one bit of advice was to "get him on tape," saying that I could have custody of the girls. One night, I'd slipped my tape recorder into the pocket of my hoodie when we went out to dinner to "discuss our options," meaning whether we would stay together or not. It was a calm and serious talk, one I was happy to have had. As I made my wants and needs known, he became upset, but stayed reasonable and was willing to repeat himself clearly enough for me to record the words: "Why don't you take the girls and move back to Ohio?" There it was, my ticket to freedom, so to speak. Little did he know, the girls were already packing little things in their "special boxes" to be kept under their beds in case we had to flee in a hurry. I had packed the tape carefully in the back of the glovebox for safekeeping, along with cash, I had been accumulating with every grocery trip and ATM visit.

On the fateful day that we were forced to leave the house, I felt ready, but not as ready as I had wanted to be. Stats ran through my mind of the number of times a woman gets the chance to leave. Any more than three and the odds of not leaving alive are drastically reduced. This had to be it, the last and final time. His behavior wasn't going to change. I'd wrongly assumed that it was his job and extracurricular activities that took over his life, and we were just "extra baggage" left to take care of ourselves. He provided the income and that was all he was capable of doing at this time.

The night in the van was uneventful. We all slept surprisingly well... when we finally did get to sleep. By the time we awoke, most of the RVs were gone, but the one shielding us from being seen from the highway was still there and offered coffee and restrooms. We thanked them for their protection and took our dopp kits into Walmart to use the restroom. By the time we came out, they were gone. I felt a sadness, as I owed them a great debt of gratitude for helping us feel safe, and offered a quick prayer for blessings and protection on their journey as well.

We grabbed a bite from Mickey D's and drove over to the camper store. As soon as we could, we loaded back up. They hitched on the trailer and reminded us of all the safety features. This time, my kiddos paid attention like never before. I think they intuitively knew they would now have more responsibility in general. I drove off the lot and, seeing another ATM, thought I could risk one last withdrawal. I would take out just under the max, so as to not trigger any alarms. Phew, the card still worked and I stowed the cash along with the rest. When I looked up, there was a sheriff's car pulling up beside me. I slowly, with a shaky hand, rolled down the window, tentatively offering, "Yes, officer?"

"Ma'am, I noticed the roll of carpet is falling off the back bumper of the camper. I wouldn't want you to lose it."

I smiled, nodded, and thanked him. He then offered to help hook it back on. The bungees had just slipped off. I declined his help, but he insisted. I tugged on that bungee so hard, with my shaky hands, that he barely noticed, but he did remark how hard it was. He tipped his hat and wished us a pleasant trip. He may have asked us where we were headed. My kids started to answer, but I informed him where my in-laws lived. Not sure they got my hint, but it kept them from telling him the full details of our itinerary.

Along the way, Hugh kept calling and leaving messages. At first they were kind, like, "Come back. It was just a misunderstanding." Then they escalated and became threats. "If you leave the state with the girls, I'll make sure you never see them again!" That one shook me to my core and had me thinking that every state trooper would have my profile and car description and chase us down. I was really scared, but still managed to stop for food and gas; I even used credit cards for the whole journey to Chicago. Looking back, I now know the motive for keeping the cards active. He was able to track each stop and know our whereabouts. In hindsight, using cash would be a safer way to travel undetected.

Our first stop was Chicago, where friends from our old church met us with an abundant outpouring of love. It reminded me of the surprise baby shower they threw for us before our first child was born, four moves ago! Joy insisted that we leave the camper down and come in to stay in the house. There was no arguing with Joy; she is that kind of a friend.

We made it to my brother's farm a day or two later. Even though he and his lovely wife offered to have us stay in the house, the girls insisted we stay in the camper, at least while the weather was nice. We were welcome to use the bathrooms and share meals with them as long as we needed. What a relief for my weary soul.

About a week later, the credit cards were cut off. No big surprise, but it was a very generous gift from Hugh, one for which I will always be grateful. He didn't want to be perceived as a bastard, or deadbeat dad. The money I stashed would hold us until a separation agreement could be arranged. In the meantime, I noticed the house I had drawn in my journal and inquired about renting it. At first, I was told it was under contract, but later found out it was going to be our new home! It was perfect for our budget and within walking distance of the kids' schools.

Kimberly Weyand is a Licensed Professional Clinical Counselor in Ohio who raised three brilliant, independent daughters as a single mom. With the strong and consistent support of many valued friends and a very close family, she kept four jobs to make ends meet. She worked as a long-term substitute teacher, an adventure course instructor, sold windows for Home Depot, and worked with her girls on a chestnut farm. When help was needed with band, speech and drama, swim team, or soccer, she dove in head-first and quickly rose to leadership. While pursuing her Master's Degree, Kimberly reluctantly gave up coaching soccer, being the president of numerous boards, including YMCA, Speech & Drama clubs, and the Water Warrior swim team. After a school crisis, her major switched from education to counseling and began a career in mental health as a case manager. Kimberly's dream is to help others build affordable homes.

The Alchemy of Spirit

BOBBI WILLIAMS

Our essence, our soul, begins to travel, float effortlessly, with the current of life, with a heightened knowing of All That Is. This knowing is intuition, and it is a gift from our soul.

Intuition

"Intuition is really a sudden immersion of the soul into the universal current of life."

–Paulo Coelho, The Alchemist

In the summer of 2012, I arrived in beautiful San Luis Obispo, California to receive certification in Soul Coaching from one of my spiritual teachers, Denise Linn. Despite my trepidation about who would be there, I courageously changed my life, just by showing up. There were women from all over the world, including Canada, England, and Norway, as well as a young Welsh man from Hong Kong.

Prior to this, my formal spiritual studies centered around Feng Shui; however, I had attended Unity Church, a metaphysical church, for a decade and was always developing my knowledge of the power of the unseen. As a little girl, I was the one who levitated friends, lit candles for comfort, and even played Ouija with my best friend for fun. Many years and books later, I found myself on this wooded ranch with psychics, shamans, angel practitioners – and I was intimidated. I was also grieving the loss of my mother eleven months prior and this ranch, with its rolling land and nature every-where, transported me to memories of my parents' beautiful home in rural Maryland, that was no longer. It was a lot to process.

Suddenly, miracles began to take place. My mother's photo ap-peared on my phone twice, though her photo was not my screen-saver. I began to cry from missing her. I believed she was sending me a sign that I was in the right place at the right time. This was the first of many synchronicities that opened my heart to appreciate my intuitive gifts and recognize the incredible gifts my peers shared.

That summer, my transformation began in earnest. I became aware of my soul's journey. I discovered the power to change my life. I opened up my intuition. I created a portal to receive the magic of the unseen. I came to the group as a questioning novice and gath-ered enough experiential evidence that my beliefs had been replaced by "knowing." Using the tarot as an analogy, I would say I traveled from The Fool – a seeker at the beginning of my journey – to the Magician, possessing a magic wand for transformation. It was my initiation to alchemy.

That journey brought me to today. I am an intuitive reader at the Edgar Cayce Center in Illinois, a Reiki Master, a Soul Coach,

Feng Shui practitioner, Certified Spiritual Counselor, and Shamanic practitioner. That summer changed the way I look at things.

Awareness is the Magic Wand

Dissolve to become something else.

"When we change the way we look at things,
the things we look at change."

~Wayne Dyer

Dyer's words deeply resonated with me, as did his explanation that alchemy is not just opening up to miracles but *expecting* them. This happens when we focus less on what we see in the physical and allow our intuitive knowing to guide us.

I recently explained to book club members that spirituality is not religion or even a belief system. It is a practice and lifestyle of Awareness that creates a Knowing. Spirituality is an everyday relationship with the Unseen. Our intuition is the lantern that leads the way to discern miracles.

The Road to the Unseen

I met Linda Drake, a psychic medium and author of *Reaching Through the Veil,* at a Mind Body Spirit fair. In my reading, she said lots of loved ones in Spirit were stepping forth. The first was "...your father, but he says he is not your father." When I told Linda he was my stepfather but I considered him a father, she replied, "He says he was not checking on you, he wanted to let you know what a good job you were doing."

I was stunned.

My father named me the executor of his trust – literally, a huge act of "trust" on his part. He was a man who kept his finances very close to him, and I was deeply moved the day he signed the papers to appoint me. I had stepsisters who were circling like vultures to receive an inheritance; plus, I had the task of relocating my parents, then in their eighties, to be near me in Chicago, and managing their expenses, the sale of their home in Maryland to an unscrupulous developer, and their day-to-day care as they aged.

My emotions were stirred almost constantly. The sale of their property involved a Chicago loan officer who lost his job because he went to extraordinary lengths to secure a five-hundred-thousand-dollar equity line for them to live on until their former home was sold. The developer in contract to buy the home changed contracts three times, prolonging the process. The hourglass was turned upside down, mounting expenses were eating away at the five hundred thousand, and my stress level was increasing daily. My father's trusted attorney colluded with the developer and made the outrageous request to "sweeten the deal" for the developer. Not happening. I remained in a mild state of panic for days, but I held down the fort without troubling my parents with the details.

After a year, my parents were running out of cash. I chose to contact a well-known attorney and auctioneering firm to let the developer know we were moving to auction if he did not complete the deal. We were two years in when, finally, the contract was executed.

My father was delighted. He passed away within the year, knowing all was taken care of.

I began the execution of the estate with those impatient, untrusting, and resentful stepsisters. I kept records of every expense to safeguard against any legal action they might take. One day, I picked up my ringing phone and was shocked when I saw my father's photo appear on the screen. The caller was my banker, Sarah, but somehow *his* photo was assigned to *her* number! I told my husband that my father was checking up on me to make sure I was taking care of business! Linda Drake's reading confirmed this, with my father coming through to communicate that, no, he was not checking, he was letting me know how proud he was!

I also noted that Linda was offering a certification course for Reiki levels I and II while she was in town. Coincidentally (actually, there are *no* coincidences in the Mind, Body, Spirit world – *synchronicity prevails)*, I had been looking for a Reiki teacher. I trained with Linda, then continued on to become a Reiki Master Teacher. Little did I know, my intuitive abilities were on the brink of skyrocketing.

Through the Veil

Our mind doesn't know the way,

Our heart has already been there,

And our soul never left.

Welcome home!

From Emmanuel's Book: *A Manual for Living Comfortably in the Cosmos*

I set up an inviting home office to receive clients for Reiki and other spiritual practices. I received a call from a woman whose elderly father was receiving chemotherapy. She worked as a physical therapist and was aware of Reiki providing healing relief to cancer patients. I booked her father for a session; she would accompany him.

As I took a shower the morning of their appointment day, I felt this overwhelming loving female energy coming to me – it was warm and exhilarating. It felt like "wife" energy, the love of a deeply familiar partner. I sensed this spirit was meant for my client.

I greeted the client and his daughter and seated them in my office for intake info. The client had a paper surgical bonnet covering his scalp. His daughter explained he had inoperable tumors on top of his head and wore the cap due to this. During intake, the older man described his daily life with his *wife* and his dog walks. Hmmm, I thought, recalling the "wife" energy that had visited me, I must have misread the energy.

After my client was placed on the massage table, I began channeling Reiki energy to him. At one point during this process, I felt the loving female energy again, this time behind my back. She was persistent and wanted me to deliver the message that she was present.

Afterward, my client sat in the chair next to his daughter, who had stayed in the room for the session. I asked how he felt and he said, "Very relaxed." I was prompted to say, "I just need to ask you, is there a woman, who was close to you, who has passed on?" He answered, "Yes, my wife," at the same time his daughter said, "My mother." I was pleased to realize that he was referring to his second wife when I collected his history; the wife energy I experienced was his *first* wife! I explained to him that her presence was with him and was incredibly warm and loving. She wanted me to speak up and tell him that she remained by his side. His daughter began to cry and said, "He took care of her when she was sick – until she passed." As they both spoke, I felt warm tingles cascading down my back, a beautiful caressing sensation, as if to say, "Thank you for letting me come through!"

This was the first time I was honored to reach through the Veil. Since then, I have experienced those "thank you" chills down my back on several other mediumship readings. Each time, I recognize this as a miracle and humbly hope it continues.

I have such gratitude for the gift of connection to Spirit!

Healing is a Simple Act

I was hospitalized for colon issues. While in bed, I turned on the TV with the remote and found a station offering sunrises filmed in hallowed locations around the world. I felt transported to Stone Henge, St Michael's Island an abandoned monastery for Celtic monks, and a Costa Rican jungle. The sun rose, birds flew and sang, the ocean rose and retreated. I witnessed the magnificent persistence of the Earth, which allowed me to surrender to the significance of my soul's purpose as well as the brevity of my life. I was at profound peace; my energy shifted.

One nurse came in and mentioned that I was the favorite patient at the nursing station.

"Your room is so serene," she said, "calm, like a spa."

I was delighted and realized that my many spiritual teachers, humans, and animals had crossed my path to show me the way to this simple act of surrender and Awareness. As the vision board in my office affirmed, *"Healing is a simple act."* Healing is, indeed, alchemy.

By taking the steps to peel back my judgments to see the existence of miracles and magic in my everyday life, my soul loved the truth that the ordinary can become mystical. I recall when my mother's photo suddenly appeared on my phone, I saw the power of my mother's love – the highest vibration – taking the ordinary photo and magically communicating to me. Once this alchemy became real, my doubts dissolved, and I began to witness and appreciate many more miracles.

Guidance to Practical Alchemy

The Elements of Transformation

To create a portal, relax, release, receive.

In a quiet place, relax with three deep breaths, release all judgments and fears and open up your heart to receive.

1. Invoke the Spirit of Air with a feather in hand. Breathe in energy from your crown chakra. Take flight with the intention of *Awareness.* Soar. Being aware that everything is energy is the first step. I have learned that being aware and witnessing without reaction or judgment is the foundation of my spiritual path. It is not deliberate, and may not always be a conscious choice, but it is seeing magic, a default Awareness.

2. Invoke the Spirit of Water, seashell in hand. Breathe in the Love that surrounds and envelops you, rest in the arms of the Divine Feminine. Pour out emotions you need to release. Imagine pouring all the tears ever shed into a Fountain and watch as they rise to the Sun. This is exquisite Forgiveness.

3. Invoke the Spirit of Fire with a pyrite crystal in hand. Breathe in a vision of a Blue Flame, walk into it, and feel the powerful purifying energy of transformation as the old rises to the Heavens and the new rises up from a grounding golden light at your feet.

4. Invoke the Spirit of Earth with a golden Amber crystal in hand. Breathe in the beauty of Mother Earth, of textures and colors, of all your senses. Know and affirm.

Behold everyday miracles and synchronicities. Seeing with new eyes, the connectedness of all things, the beauty of all of Nature, the healing energy of our planet, all people, all colors. Give gratitude to the Creator from your heart. A portal is now open to discern Alchemy.

"I have been and still am a seeker, but I have ceased to question stars and books; I have begun to listen to the teaching my blood whispers to me."

–Hermann Hesse

Listen to your intuition. It is the voice of your soul. It is the lantern that reveals your own Alchemy.

☾

Bobbi Williams grew up in Chicago, Illinois. Her parents had books by Edgar Cayce and psychic phenomena, and they spoke openly about such topics and the meaning of life. However, it wasn't until later that Bobbi's interest in spirituality began to surface. Since then, she has become a Spiritual Counselor through the American Institute of Healthcare Professionals and a Reiki Master Teacher. She has also studied Shamanism and Feng Shui. Her chapter in *The Wild Woman's Book of Shadows* (under the pseudonym Esme Chamane) was her first published work, followed by chapters in *Wild Woman's Book of Prosperity* and *Navigating the Pandemic: Stories of Hope and Resilience*. Bobbi has taught numerous spiritual classes at Unity Northwest and gives intuitive readings at the Edgar Cayce Center for Research and Enlightenment. You can learn more at:

home4thesoul.com

Journey from Fear to Freedom

BECKY WOODS

"There's a freedom waiting for you, on the breezes of the
sky, and you ask, 'What if I fall?' Oh, but darling,
what if you fly?"

~ Erin Hanson

Looking back, I believe it was the anger that fueled me and pushed me through my fear. You see, my life had changed within a matter of months. First, I was notified that I was getting laid off. Two weeks later, without notice, my husband moved out, taking two of our four kids. I had bills to pay and kids to feed! Meanwhile, we were all trying to adjust to our family being ripped in half and our worlds turned upside down. I was really confused, overwhelmed, heartbroken, and angry. Angry at myself for failing as a parent, angry at my ex, and at men in general. If you were a man and crossed my path back then, God help you!

I had an associate's degree in healthcare and even that wasn't enough to pay all the bills. I wasn't afraid to work, but who would take care of my kids? I needed a good schedule, one that allowed me to be home every night; however, in my line of work, if you wanted to earn a good wage, you worked at a hospital, stayed onsite two nights a week, and rotated weekends. I thought I was going to have to ask my mom if we could move in with her. I felt lost, desperate, and defeated – like a total loser!

Then I started thinking of how unfair it was that men were able to support themselves and their kids on one salary. That's when it hit me! I needed a "man's" job so I could earn a "man's" wage! I was determined to find a job and keep my family afloat! By God, if a man could do it, then, dammit, so could I!

A local farmer agreed to let me try driving one of his trucks for sugar beet harvest. After a couple of quick lessons from friends and family, I was off to haul sugar beets! I was nervous! I didn't want to embarrass myself or ruin this guy's truck. Turns out I had nothing to worry about. Harvest was a success, plus, I actually enjoyed the work! I decided to take the commercial driver's license test, and I passed! This was the start of my truck driving career. I was officially working in a man's occupation in a man's world for a man's wage! I learned how to haul everything from dirt to hot asphalt! I was working long days, often six days a week, *but* I was home every night for my kids. Driving is a physically taxing job. You don't just drive around all day, like in your car. It was really hard and I did it! I did it for six years.

There was nothing *equal* about working in an occupation that requires physical labor and is dominated by males. I was seen as a nuisance, dismissed, ignored, and taunted the whole time. I thought if I got really good at my job I could earn some respect. It didn't matter. Men with no experience were hired at five dollars more an hour than women with twenty years of experience. That fueled my anger even more.

I started asking myself, "What would a man do?"

A man would be aggressive and go to the boss and complain! He would demand more money, otherwise he would quit and go somewhere else. The new guys getting hired negotiated their wages. Have you heard about the squeaky wheel? It gets the grease. Since they thought I was a pain in the ass already, I figured I'd dial it up a notch and I became *really* squeaky. It was exhausting and I wanted to give up so many times. I didn't. I averaged about a dollar raise each year! That was much better than my 2.5% cost-of-living wage increases in healthcare, plus, the insurance was paid for and much better. I learned to negotiate! I built my confidence and became comfortable asking for more.

I had many falls both literally and figuratively! My house was in pre-foreclosure for almost two years. Two *effing* years! Many times, the thought crossed my mind that I should just let it go. My ex-husband was still on the loan, so he would have the option to take it over. I wasn't going to let him have my house! My mortgage payment was cheaper than an apartment and my credit was crap so I couldn't even get an apartment if I had the money.

Then there was the finalizing of the divorce, trying online dating (epic fail); I drank a lot that first year! I wasn't a good mom for the first couple of years, and it showed.

While I felt like I was winning in some areas, I felt like I was failing miserably in others. I dumped loads of gravel in the wrong places. I backed into a parked pickup. I almost took out a power line. One time, I even put the wrong kind of diesel fuel in my truck.

I finally got my house out of pre-foreclosure and one kid off to college. Then peri-menopause decided to visit! For real! I can't make this shit up! So now I'm bouncing around in my truck with diapers on all day, every day! Not cool (literally)!

That fall, we had an ice storm. I was already having trouble with the steering on my truck. No one believed me. I finally told them I wasn't driving it anymore. So they said, "Okay, we will find someone who 'can' drive it and you can go home. I said "Fine!" and left. Needless to say, I was second-guessing myself all the way home because I felt like I still didn't have enough experience. I did know that something had changed in the way my truck was handling, though, and I didn't feel safe. Turns out, the man who drove it also noticed something wasn't right. It finally went into the shop and they found out it had a broken tie-rod. That's a big deal! I felt a little more confident after that. The mechanic always said that when I brought my truck in, there was always something legit wrong. Building confidence takes time.

Later that winter, I was hauling out to the lakes area with curvy roads and steep hills. The truck was fully loaded, with sixteen tons of gravel. Long story short, I didn't make it up a hill but slid backward, headed right for the lake. Somehow, I got it stopped before we got there. When I stepped out of the truck, I fell on my ass and slid all the way down the hill. I shouldn't have been out driving that day in the first place, but miles equal money! That's a man's world for ya!

When I got laid off for the winter, I scheduled a hysterectomy. Shortly after my surgery, I found out I had developed Hashimoto's, an autoimmune disease. I was tired, and I was tired of this work. I had offers from other companies and many compliments, so I knew I had become a good driver. Still, I asked the Universe for an easier job for the same amount of money or more. I felt like I didn't have much fight left in me! I was constantly working and always tired. My anger was gone. I was just worn out!

Around the same time, a friend of mine called and asked if I'd consider coming back to work at a rural hospital. She also mentioned that they had just revamped the wage scales, increasing them considerably. I hesitated; after all, I had been out of the healthcare field for almost eight years and wasn't sure I could catch back up. Then I thought, *What can it hurt?* As a bonus, this manager used to be a teacher at the local tech! I figured that would be a great person to get me back up to speed. I applied and they offered me the job with a sign-on bonus! Are you ready for the best part? The wage was nine dollars more an hour than my driving wage, and thirteen dollars more an hour than I was making when I left my clinic job. This meant I could say goodbye to physical labor and only work just four eight-hour days a week!

The first year was hard. So much had changed in the healthcare field that I felt like I was starting from square one. I made mistakes. I had some falls. I didn't give up, though, and I was soon at the top of my game again!

Then Covid hit...

What a hellish time in healthcare. I started taking more online classes and joining different healing groups. I was home more to help with online high school. I went back on an antidepressant drug! I upgraded my self-care routine. After a few years, I was able to re-finance my mortgage for a lower interest rate and get the house in my name only! That really felt like an accomplishment. I was finally free of my ex!

My life started to change with my youngest graduating and grandkids on the way. My dream had always been to own my own business. I started working on it, taking classes, and getting business cards. I authored a chapter in a compilation book, and it became an Amazon bestseller! I learned how to do social media and manage my own website. I started posting some videos on YouTube. I got certified in a few natural healing modalities. I was taking steps, but I didn't feel like I had enough time to dedicate to it. I started asking the Universe for a job that paid the same or more for fewer hours so I could work on building my business. I wasn't getting any younger! Wouldn't you know it, I heard about a job that was exactly what I was looking for. They offered me a sign-on bonus as well, with a two-year commitment! Now that I wasn't afraid to negotiate, I asked for double the bonus with a one-year commitment – and I got it! Now I have time to grow my business! Soon, I plan to work my business full time.

About four years ago, I took what I call a "fun risk" – I bought a Harley Davidson! I hadn't taken a class yet and couldn't even drive the motorcycle home – I had a friend do that for me. I took the class a couple of weeks later and now I am an official "wind sister!" I told myself that if I could learn to drive a truck, I could learn to ride a motorcycle! Let me tell you, there is no feeling of freedom like going down the open road with the wind in your hair! If I can learn to ride a motorcycle at forty-five, I think I can learn to do anything!

That's how it works. You take one little scary step at a time toward your desires. You do it afraid. You survive! You build confidence. You do the next hard thing. You succeed. You build more confidence! It's a snowball effect. You might not go jump in a truck like I did, but start doing the little things that are scary and eventually you will work your way up to the bigger things. This is how you alchemize fear into freedom! Soon things won't seem scary, just uncomfortable. Then, before you know it, they won't seem uncomfortable. They will seem exciting! Then you will be free and unstoppable. Free to do, have, or create anything you desire!

I no longer believe in the lines that separate occupations into men's and women's. I am no longer a man-hater. I am working on creating healthy relationships.

I believe men and women have access to both feminine and masculine energy. Men can tap into their feminine energy to be more nurturing and compassionate. Women can tap into their masculine energy and to be more assertive and more confident in negotiating. We need to tap into it and learn how to use it. It is our birthright. When we can have a true balance of both, we will thrive and we will be free!

What if you fall? Oh darling, but what if you fly? Are you ready and willing to risk falling down a couple of times for a chance to fly? Are you ready to be free from fear? If I can do it, so can you. Just take that first small, scary step. Do it afraid. You got this!

Sending you so much love and courage on your journey! It's never too late. Remember, the younger generations are watching and learning from us. Let's teach them how it's done!

☽

Women and their overall health and wellbeing are Becky's passions. She facilitates women's gatherings and believes that women are meant to come together to grow, celebrate, grieve, learn, heal, and thrive. She is an Intuitive Energy Coach. Becky has a special place in her heart for veterans and their families as well as children and our elders. She weaves inner child, past life, shadow work, generational, and multidimensional healing into her sessions. She is a medium and invites her spirit guide team to guide her. Becky's goal is to create a safe sacred space for you. Only when you feel totally safe are you able to be vulnerable, and that's when you are able to make the most progress on your self- care and healing journey. To learn more about opportunities to work with her, check out her website:

energeezinc.com

The Magic of Moon Alchemy

TAMMY ZAYAC

Have you heard the quote, "The only thing constant in life is change"? Well, I would like to add the MOON to that quote. It has been a guidepost in the sky for millennia, and when we attune to the moon, a practice rooted in mindfulness and mysticism, we cultivate deeper self-awareness, spiritual growth, healing, and transformation … AND it's really fun!

The moon promotes the idea that we can have flow within a cyclical structure. As someone who loves structure and cycles, I have found harmonizing with the moon to be a beautiful way to navigate my day-to-day, cultivate positive expectancy, practice self-care, heal trust wounds, and stay soulfully grounded and centred. It has helped me in creating a life of peace, balance, freedom, and authenticity.

I have found that every month, with every lunar cycle, we are given the opportunity to tune into the ebb and flow of subtle but powerful moon energy to RELEASE, RESTORE, RESET & RISE.

I invite you to follow and flow with me as I journey through a moon cycle. An alchemical cycle aiding in transmutation, transformation, and manifestation.

I'll start at the RELEASE phase of the cycle, because when we release, we make space and, with space, we can create.

RELEASE

Energetic release is amazing for healing and aligning with our higher purpose, and there is no better time to release than at the full moon. We have been practicing ritual and ceremony for centuries or more at the full moon, tapping into its magic, power, and potent healing energy. Some like to gather with like-minded souls to share in the magic. And some, like myself, enjoy it as a solo act.

When I say ritual or ceremony, I really just mean a mindful practice that creates space to honour ourselves, the moon, and our higher source. It can be elaborate or simple, long or short. There is no right or wrong, so do what feels authentic and comfortable for you.

In my practice, I start by creating a quiet space often the night before the full moon peaks. I light a candle, centre and ground myself, ask for guidance, and have paper and pen ready.

As I write, I imagine the moonlight illuminating what is no longer working for me and my highest good. I intend to release, let go, and move away from all that is completed, blocking, or stopping forward movement in my life. Whether that be mindset, people, places, situations, wounds, patterns, or limiting beliefs that cause me to stop, stagnate, or feel lost, I allow it all to be shown trusting that it is ready to be released.

This is also a great time to forgive. Let's talk about the word "forgive," because it can shut us down if we don't remember that forgiveness is medicine and a gift to ourselves that clears clutter, heals wounds, and empowers us. Furthermore, forgiveness doesn't confront, condone, or forget anything or anyone. It is not meant to minimize our feelings or the situation, and it *definitely* does not mean we have to welcome anything or anyone back into our life if we don't want to. Forgiveness is also not time-sensitive, so I encourage everyone to honour their own pace.

Furthermore, we are worthy and deserving of all the self-forgiveness we can manage, so please include yourself on your list.

As you can see, I am passionate about the power of forgiveness! It's a game-changer, like having a dose of needed medicine on a consistent basis. This is why I love to include it in my full moon practice.

Once I am done writing I burn the paper, watch the flames, and imagine it all being sent off to be transmuted into the ethers with love and gratitude. I say something like, "Thank you (to the moon, my guides, my source) for shining the light on all that is no longer serving. I am grateful for the lessons and the wisdom gained. I am ready to release, let go, and forgive anything and everything that isn't for my highest good."

I then write a gratitude list. Energetically, space is being made, and I want to fill that space with higher vibes before any low-vibe thoughts or energies can seep in. I write out all that brings me peace, joy, appreciation, and gratitude. It's a bit like a soothing balm for the mind, body, and soul.

I also charge my crystals, say a forgiveness mantra under the moonlight and, when I feel inclined, I make moon water.

Other RELEASE tips:

- Remember to be specific about what is being released and forgiven.

- There can be layers of healing, so it isn't always a one-and-done process but we have many full moons to work with.

- Consider pulling oracle or tarot cards and ask self-reflective questions. Trust what comes in.

- Allow emotions to flow – they can be cathartic and a sign of release and healing.

- We can also look at astrology and see what zodiac sign is flavouring the energy of the full moon. This can guide us to become aware of a life aspect that needs some releasing and forgiving attention.

RESTORE

After the full moon we enter the waning phase of the moon cycle, which is conducive to our Mind-Body-Soul RESTORATION. It can be a lot of work releasing, forgiving, and creating space!

During this phase, allow for a little solitude and self-reflection, then ask your mind, body, and soul, "What do I need right now for restoration?" Trust what comes in and then go about trying to make it happen with no pressure or urgency. Maybe it's journaling, resting, sleeping, yoga, movement, clutter clearing, ten minutes of sunshine, or five minutes of stillness. Whatever you are being called to do, try to make it happen during this week-and-a-half-long phase.

Find ways in your days to RESTORE.

Third Quarter moon (aka half-moon) is next in the waning phase, where we are invited to have an attitude of gratitude. My gratitude practice includes writing the "long" list – BIG or small; I write it all. I tap into what is working in my life, what I appreciate, who I am thankful for, all that brings me peace and makes me smile. Having gratitude, appreciation, and thankfulness energy activates the universal law of attraction. Energy flows where focus goes, and what we put out, we get back.

RESET

Who doesn't love a good reset!? The darkness right before the new moon feels like a long push and hold of the pause button – the reset before the clarity.

My new moon practice is similar to that of the full moon, except I am in manifesting mode instead of releasing mode, and I do my practice on the day/night after the new moon appears. At this time, I open my mind and bring in curiosity, listen to my heart and bring in truths, connect to my soul, and ask what goals, dreams, desires, and longings are wanting to be communicated. I then start to write and create what I like to call the "empowered list."

I allow the dreams, desires, and goals to come up and out because the awareness and clarity are the first steps to manifesting them. This practice sets a powerful intention and ultimately is letting the Universe know that I am open and ready to co-create.

Other RESET tips:

- Stay curious, there may be blocks and triggers and that's okay – just make note of what they are. We are only planting the seeds for our future – there is no pressure to change everything all at once and overcome all the hurdles on this moon. It's a process, and with moon synchronizing we are guided through it.

- If you process better with the spoken word, you can speak it as you write or record yourself.

- Again, we can look at astrology and see what zodiac sign is flavouring the energy of the new moon. This can be a guide to which life aspect needs some moon-manifesting attention.

- Let the senses take over. What would it feel, smell, taste, and look like? Really allow yourself to see, feel, and be in the intended manifestation.

RISE

As we enter the waxing phase of the moon cycle, there is a gentle momentum, and I see it as a time to tap into the growing and expanding energy. I look at the empowered list and decide which one(s) I want to move forward on. Then I rise up on an energetic, physical, and spiritual level and take some grounded and inspired action towards the goal(s).

I break the steps down into bite-sized, digestible, and sustainable actions. For example, If I want to travel, I start by making "the travel list": research the area, check out flights, and set up an automatic savings plan. Or if I am looking for more peace in my life, I start by allowing curiosity to lead, use word medicine, clutter clear, have a look at different aspects of my life, and find books, mentors, and/or teachers that resonate.

Other RISE tips:

- As you rise, remember to be gentle with yourself and honour your pace and nervous system.

- Remember that you have a chance every month to do this, so try to focus on one or two items on your list.

- Please believe that you are worthy and deserving of all that is meant for you – embody the energy of "I will see it when I BELIEVE it."

- Always remember to step out of your own way. Often, we can block our progress because of a worthiness or trust wound – observe without judgment.

- The power of intention and the law of detachment go a long way.

As we cruise along the waxing phase, we come to the first quarter moon (aka half-moon), which is another gentle reminder to do the gratitude practice again.

A few days after the first quarter moon I like to take stock...reassess, revisit, and maybe revise my empowered list. Sometimes, as we take the inspired steps, "things" can come up and challenge us. This is because when we state to the Universe what we want, what we *don't* want comes to the surface to be cleared. When we "stir the pot," and possibly disturb the status quo, things can start to feel out of balance.

Biggest tip here is to take note, lean in, listen to your body, and follow the triggers – they can tell us so much.

At the waxing gibbous phase, a few days out from the full moon, it is a potent time to start the RELEASE process again. As the moon grows, so too can the emotions. I tend to feel all the feels and can be overwhelmed by them during this time. So, if you are feeling wobbly or finding that your emotions are cluttering up your energy field, have a look at the following self-care practice that can prepare you for the full moon.

Rant & Rave (Expressive) Journaling:

FEEL IT, WRITE IT, BURN IT, AND RELEASE IT.

- Centre yourself and have pen and paper ready.

- Tap in – feel the feels and acknowledge it all.

- Write out all grievances – anything that comes to the surface.

- No sugarcoating or spiritualizing – write everything as is.

- When finished, burn the paper (s) right away.

- Let it all go while the fire transmutes the energy into the ethers.

- Repeat as necessary

This isn't about spiritual bypassing; it's about keeping it real and allowing the emotions to be FELT and FLOW through us. The unedited "beefs" are up and out and not sticking onto anyone else. It's like clutter-clearing for clarity; it sets us up for next-level release and healing at the full moon.

As you can see, moon alchemy is a wash, rinse, and repeat process. It is a cycle of contraction and expansion. There is emotional, energetic, and sometimes physical release, self-reflection, intention-setting, and inspired action, with gratitude and appreciation weaved throughout. This alchemy teaches us to BALANCE the light and the shadow, TRUST our journey, ALLOW curiosity, flow, and acceptance, and BELIEVE we can create a life by design. Furthermore, there is no right or wrong to this process, and you can do it using my practice as a guideline.

If you fall off the moon cycle, that's okay! Jump back in any time. Remember, it's our constant, our anchor, and our guide; it meets us right where we're at with no judgment and no expectation of perfection.

If we let it, the moon, just like the Universe, strives to conspire with us instead of against us. It shows us that we are whole, no matter what phase we are in. May you believe that for yourself.

Moon Blessings to You

May you be open to receive the magical, healing, and empowering energy of the moon. And may moon alchemy help you live in flow, balance, peace, freedom, and harmony while uncovering and discovering your true-to-you, authentic self. So be it.

Tammy Zayac runs an online business as the Intuitive Guide-By-Your-Side and journeys with and empowers women of all ages and stages to cultivate PEACE in their body and mind, uncover their AUTHENTIC self, and learn to TRUST their journey.

She is an empowered empath, travel enthusiast, a creative, a moon and clutter-clearing alchemist, and a self-proclaimed **Woman in Progress (W.I.P.).**

She believes that when we can live more curious and less serious, and accept and honour the who, what, why, and how of us, we have the recipe for living an empowered, peaceful, and authentic life. You can find her at:

tammyzayac.ca

Thank you for reading our stories, hearing our words, and embracing our rituals. Thank you for awakening the wild woman and fueling her passion and desire to express, create, and live a mystical life rich with community and sisterhood. Together we rise and celebrate each woman — WE ALL GET TO WIN.

☾

www.ingramcontent.com/pod-product-compliance
Lightning Source LLC
Chambersburg PA
CBHW071719120626
46550CB00001B/307